"Leslie Sann has laid out before us,

in this one colorful, readable book,

the true power tools of an enlightened

consciousness. I wish I'd had this book

thirty years ago!"

Steve Chandler

Author of *Time Warrior*

꙼ꙮ

"Knowing Leslie as long as I do, I know

that everything in this book has been tested through

her experience. I'm certain that anyone dipping into

these simple ideas and easily practiced skills will find

their life joyfully enriched."

H. Ronald Hulnick, Ph.D,

Co-author of

Loyalty To Y
The Heart of Spin

LIFE HAPPENS

What Are YOU

Going to Do About It?

To Jinc & Catherine,
Blessings,
Leslie Sann

LIFE HAPPENS

What Are YOU
Going to Do About It?

a practical handbook with
Powerful Tools to Access
Your Inner Resources and
Transform Your Life

LESLIE SANN

Life Happens

What Are YOU Going to Do About It?

For permission requests, write to the publisher, at the e-mail address below.

Living by Design Press
leslie@living-bydesign.com

ISBN-13:
978-0692443637 (Living by Design Press)

ISBN-10:
0692443630

Dedicated to John-Roger

who led the way to my heart,

and is the inspiration for my work.

Table of Contents

Preface

Imagine life filled with possibilities because you know what to do when life throws you a curve ball. Imagine moving from victim to victorious because you respond to life circumstances rather than react. Imagine what you could do, create, have, be, because you trust your creativity and inner resources and know, no matter what happens, you will find a way to win.

It is my heart's desire to leave the world better than I found it. One of the ways I do this is by helping people change the way they experience who they are and what they can do. Through our work, they are empowered to create a life they love and be the person they love. They learn to live by design and thus transform their lives.

I consider it a privilege and a blessing to be part of the process of transformation in the lives of my clients. This book contains some of the most powerful transformational tools and practices that I teach.

I have discovered these tools throughout the course of my life, mostly from being off course, falling down and figuring out how to stand back up again and stay up longer. I have learned falling down is a gift, for it brings an opportunity to grow into places I haven't yet been. I may not like the falling down part but I like the getting back up, growing into a stronger me. This book is sourced from my desire to share what I have learned from my experience of what doesn't work and discovering what does.

Trust me, I am very human, just like you. I have had my share of hardship and heartbreak, as well as good fortune and blessings. I use the practices I am sharing. They have changed my life. They continue to change my life, moment-to-moment, breath-by-breath. They are my gift to you.

Introduction

YOU have the power to transform yourself and your life. When life does what it does ... do something back. Use this book to help you do so. Don't just read it, DO it. *Use* it to empower yourself to do what it takes to change your life, so that rather than living by default, you are living by design - by choice, rather than by chance.

Powerful people live by design. Living by design is living mindfully on purpose, sourced from love and compassion, making choices and taking action to create a happy, joyful life.

Reading about life isn't the same as living it. Experiment with my suggestions. Discover for yourself what works FOR YOU. Doing is key. Action changes lives. Don't take my word for it. Check it out.

As you empower yourself with your *choices* and *actions,* you may discover an inner joy that comes with using your creative energies, to craft the life you want. Joyful people think differently, are more inventive, resilient, patient, generous, optimistic and kind. They focus more on what IS working rather than what is not, fostering gratitude and even more joy, because what is uncovered is a good experience to live in. In the goodness, there is joy. In the joy, there is ease.

In the ease, there is power.

Just as a carpenter uses power tools to make the work easier, powerful people use Power Tools. No matter how big the obstacles have been in my life, using the Power Tools I am about to share with you has enabled me to transform stumbling blocks into stepping stones, lifting me into an expanded sense of purpose and empowerment, thus making whatever I'm facing easier to navigate.

Mastery in life is not about avoiding adversity or challenges. It is about learning life skills, so that you are resilient, responsive and resourceful when life does what it does. It is about embracing change while learning, so you can meet life on life's terms and win.

This book is here for you. Do it the way you want. You can pick up the book, look at the table of contents, choose a chapter and begin. You may read the book in the order I have laid it out. You could even open the book randomly and see what is there for you. All I ask is that you read the first chapter before you get into the rest of the book. Promise?

Some of the chapters have a suggestion of something to do. I've entitled those sections, *'Do This ...'* After all, this *is* a practical handbook, which means it is here for you to put to use. Practice the skills and apply the tools, tools that will make your life easier.

Occasionally, you will come across a *'Hmm ...'* followed by words to provoke deeper consideration. These are questions to ponder. I sometimes call them wonder questions. I encourage you to read the question and let it simmer. You could say the question aloud, starting with hmm. It has been proven that when we hum the sound vibrates both the left and the right brain, creating a whole brain access.

Perhaps, set a timer for 3 minutes. Write what is present for you. See what you uncover. Or you could chew on the question throughout the day and jot down your insights in your nighttime journal if you keep one. *The more you know about what is true for you, the more you can fine-tune the design of your life.*

Let this book change you. Better said, *change yourself* by making good use of this book. The tools and practices I'm about to share are simple and life changing ... if you use them.

And now, we begin a journey to a more empowered you...

1. Powerful People Make Things Easy

*It's easier to act your way into a new way of
thinking, than to think your way into a new
way of acting.*

Millard Fuller

๑ß

Years ago, I was participating in a ropes course adventure training. One of the events involved climbing way, way up a very tall tree on a rope ladder, stopping to balance on a small board. Once stabilized on the board, the task was to jump off, the goal a trapeze. If successful, one would be gripping the bar, hanging in the air, 30 feet above the ground.

Not all attempts were successful.

Successful or not, there was a fall to earth, either from the platform or the trapeze.

We were belayed, meaning we were connected to a rope someone on the ground was holding securely. When we let go of the trapeze or missed it completely, a bungee type rope would bounce us high enough above the ground so we could safely be guided back to earth.

Clearly, in order to jump from the platform, we had to trust the safety ropes.

I was part of a group of 8 people. We each took turns climbing the tree and jumping. Some of the group members were a bit anxious. Others were downright terrified. I, on the other hand, was eager to go.

It was my turn. Up the rope ladder, I climbed. Halfway to the top, George (the man holding the ladder steady for me) decided to make my trip up a bit more challenging, so he let go.

Marvelous.

Suddenly the journey up wasn't so easy. The rope ladder began to wobble. What I was doing was no longer working. I felt the heat of anger.

I paused, took a breath and faced the new circumstances. How was I going to get to the top, without George anchoring me into the earth? (Pausing to take a breath consciously is a good choice at times like this.)

Using the anger energy as fuel, I shoved my feet further beyond the rungs of the ladder into the tree trunk and pulled myself to the top, using the tree to support me onward and upward. Once on the top, I balanced myself on the itty-bitty piece of wood used as a perch. As I began to turn around, so that I could leap for the bar, George (my new friend), challenged me to fall backward.

The challenge? To let go of going for the goal, the trapeze, and fall into the unknown, blind to where I was going. My initial thought was that it was too easy. What was the point if I wasn't going to go for the goal, jump for the ring, making my mark through ambition and striving?

Another pause, another breath.

I decided to do it. I said *"yes"* to the challenge to let go of the challenge.

I turned around, arms crossed over my chest, brought my heels to the edge of the board, leaned back slowly and fell backwards through the air.

The ropes caught me.

I bounced and swung until one of the assistants steadied me, congratulated me, and asked how I was doing.

I was shaking all over. Every cell of my body was vibrating. I was whirling with energy. I answered her inquiries with, *"that was easy,"* my critical mind wanting to negate what just occurred, telling me if it were easy it didn't count.

She spoke something that has stayed with me all these years. She looked me in the eyes and said, *"Powerful people make things easy."*

"Powerful? Me?"

I later found myself wondering, *"What about me made that easy? What was I doing, thinking, and acting differently than those who were struggling?"* These questions have fueled much curiosity over the years. The following pages contain some of the many Power Tools I have uncovered. I invite you to put them to good use.

ℬ ℬ ℬ ℬ ℬ ℬ ℬ ℬ

Hmm ...

How is it YOU are powerful?

ℬ ℬ ℬ ℬ ℬ ℬ ℬ ℬ

2. Envision This

If you don't know where you are going, any road will do and you probably won't get there.

Unknown

৵৶

I knew where I was going. I was climbing to the top of the tree. I was clear, focused and ascending with purpose. Even though George let go of the ladder and I was momentarily disrupted in my process, I reoriented myself, found a new way to make what I wanted happen and kept taking one step after another, until I reached the platform.

That wasn't the goal. That was just part of the process. The goal was to complete the exercise. Climb to the top, jump off, or for some of us, me in particular, the task was to fall backwards. I had a new goal, new choices, new actions, and new alignment with a purpose.

Oh, purpose ... what was the purpose of the exercise? To face a challenge, to meet adversity and to come back to home – earth. We expand and then we come back to ourselves. We go out into the world, we have experiences and then we bring them home, no longer the same as we were, now expanded with new experience, new growth, occurring through new opportunity.

When you are powerful in your life, you meet adversity, call upon inner resources, learn new things, complete your experience and come back again. Each segment of the journey has a vision, a purpose and a direction that keeps you moving forward.

Whenever you feel lost, out of sorts, disconnected, you might ask yourself, *"Do I know where I'm going? What do I want? What outcome am I moving toward? What is the experience I want to create for myself?"*

There is a Japanese proverb saying, *"A vision without action is a daydream. Action, without vision, is a nightmare."* We want to turn our dreams into reality and we do that by having vision and taking action.

☙ ❧ ☙ ❧ ☙ ❧ ☙ ❧

Hmm ...

Where are you going?

☙ ❧ ☙ ❧ ☙ ❧ ☙ ❧

3. Action, Action, Action

You'll never plough a field by turning it over in your mind.

Irish Proverb

❧

Do you remember learning about inertia in school? How an object at rest tends to stay at rest, unless acted upon by an outside force? That's what is going on when a person feels stuck in their life. They're not moving in a direction they want to go.

For example, one of the women who participated in the ropes course got half way up the ladder and froze. She wouldn't move up and she wouldn't come back down. She was stuck. There she was on the ladder, halfway up, halfway down and not choosing to go in either direction.

Perhaps her big brother teased her when she was little about being a girl and now is timid about doing things when men are watching. Or maybe something happened and now she has a fear of heights, or perhaps ... Guess what? It really doesn't matter. Figuring out a problem gives you a well-analyzed problem. She is still half way up the tree. It is getting dark and the temperature is dropping.

The key is to get unstuck and back in the flow of life. Moving in the direction we want to go is to make a choice and take an action. She could choose up, or down. This is where our true power lies.

The word power comes from the French word 'pouvoir' meaning to be able. As defined in Webster's, it is the ability to do, the capacity to act, capability of performing or producing.

Power is an assessment about a person's capacity to generate action. Action produces results. Therefore, power is the ability to do something, to make choices, take action and produce results.

That's it.

I bet you can find many places in your life where you are powerful, where you are competent in producing results.

Perhaps, like me, you tend not to notice because it is easy for you.

When we are in our power, there is ease.

Perhaps you thought being powerful was accompanied by a lot of grunting, pushing, and struggle. I did, until I fell backwards out of a tree.

Power has ease as it is sourced from action. Climb to the top of the rope ladder, fall backwards ... write a book. Got it?

Next time you are stuck, remember the movie director's cry: ACTION!

✿ ❧ ✿ ❧ ✿ ❧ ✿ ❧

Hmm ...

Wonder about the statement:

"Powerful people make things easy."

✿ ❧ ✿ ❧ ✿ ❧ ✿ ❧

4. Do More of What Works

The secret of success? Fall down seven times.
Get up eight.

Chinese Proverb

༚༚

A simple definition of success: Do more of what works, less of what doesn't and experiment with new things. Observation is powerful. As we notice what is working, we know to do more of that. Noticing what isn't working is an encouragement to do something else. Simple. Do more of what works, less of what doesn't and experiment with alternatives.

Since I am a naturally coordinated, physically capable person, when faced with climbing the tree, my self-talk was filled with *"I can do this."* I can only guess what the others in my group were saying to themselves. Perhaps those who were afraid, were telling themselves a story that was frightening, such as, *"I'm gonna die!"* Not a great motivator for getting on the ladder.

There are areas in my life where I am not as confident. I struggle when my self-talk is full of doubt, my own version of *"I'm gonna die!"* The result of self-doubt is inaction, or action poorly done resulting in creating evidence that supports the story of 'I doubt I can'.

Hmm, based on results doubt is not working for me. Time to change my approach. I could experiment in reminding myself I CAN succeed, IF I am willing to participate. Maybe not the first time, yet based on personal history, I know I learn from experience. This gives me the confidence to take the actions and learn what I need to, in order to make what I want happen. I have accessed my power. Much better, yes?

If you are doing something that isn't working, no big deal. Just stop it and play with something else. Keep experimenting until you discover what works and then do more of that. Keep doing that until it doesn't work for you anymore. And have fun!

Climbing the rope ladder worked for me until George let go. I then had to find a new way of doing. Life is like that. Things change. As Chaung Tzu said a long time ago, in 300 B.C., *"The only thing constant in life is change."* We do until our doing isn't doing it for us anymore and then we do something else.

୬ଙ ୬ଙ ୬ଙ

Do This ... Notice, Learn, Do

- Take time to notice where you find ease in your life. Observe what you are doing, how you are doing it, as well as what you are saying to yourself or to others, that facilitates this ease. [Hint: Ease may look like smiling, relaxed shoulders, quick to laughter, humor, easy breathing …]

- Pay attention to where you find struggle. Become aware of your actions and your talk. See if you can discover how you might be contributing to the unease. [Hint: Struggle may be associated with rushing, multi-tasking, short fuse, tight shoulders and jaw, impatience, anxiety …

- Can you learn from what is easy in your life and apply some of those tools to where you are struggling? Play with new ways of doing.

- Keep playing, experimenting and having fun doing what you do, so that you can have what you want.

5. Try Harder – N o t

This summer has seen the completion of the 1860s farmhouse project. It has taken us three years to renovate the structure but we now have moved across the driveway. Dreams do come true with enough determination, patience and hard work. Next year we tackle the barn.

Penny Newkirk

༉༄

Okay, check this out. Find something within your reach right now that is easily picked up.

NOTICE it with your eyes.

Now THINK the thought, *"I'm going to pick that up."*

Now IMAGINE yourself picking the item up.

FEEL the emotions you experience when you successfully achieve something you set out to do.

Great.

Now TRY to pick it up.

If the item is in your hand right now you didn't TRY, so set it down.

Now TRY to pick it up.

I want you to really try HARD.

Try HARDER!

Ahhh, if you picked it up you failed at trying, even if you tried harder, so set it back down.

Okay. Now PICK IT UP.

If you have the item in your hand, you DID it! You picked it up. You took an action and created a result.

Thinking about doing something does not make it happen. Imagining doing something doesn't do it either. Feeling like doing it doesn't work. Trying – well – TRY to pick it up.

Trying is not doing. Experimenting is also not trying. Experimenting is committing to a course of ACTION without being sure of the outcome. When we experiment, we assess a situation, decide a best next action, take that action and then observe the result. Did it get us closer to the goal? If yes, do more. If no, experiment with a different action.

Action is what produces results. We can pretend we are taking action by telling ourselves we tried, or we're thinking about it, or imagining our success, but as the Nike ad says, *"DOING does it!"*

ℰ ℒ ℰ ℒ ℰ ℒ ℰ ℒ

Hmm ...

When someone says they will try to arrive to
pick you up at the airport at the time
you asked them, does that engender trust in
you? What does 'try' actually mean?
Can you count on it?
Is it reliable?

ℰ ℒ ℰ ℒ ℰ ℒ ℰ ℒ

6. Who Did That?

Genuine responsibility – the kind that changes
your life – does not begin until you take it.

Gay Hendricks

๛

Let's pretend you and I are in the same room physically. Now imagine me asking your permission to touch your forearm and you say, *"Yes."* I reach out and gently press my finger onto your arm and ask you what you notice. You look at your arm as I pull my hand away and say:

"Leslie, there is a spot on my arm where your finger was."

It is true. I have touched your arm gently and as I take my hand away, we both see a dot appear where my finger was.

I now ask you, *"Who did that?"*

If you are like most people, you will reply:

"You did that, Leslie. You made the spot."

Hmm, but what if I reach out and touch the arm of the chair you are sitting on? Perhaps the top of your shoe? What happens?

N o t h i n g a t a l l.

The pigment of the chair cloth and your shoe remains as it was.

So, I ask you again, who made the temporary mark on your arm?

The answer is you, dear reader. You made the mark. Your body responded to my touch. My finger triggered the reaction of your body, but your body 'did' it.

So what? Why does this matter if you want to be an empowered person living by design?

Well, if I DID IT you are a victim to the perturbance of my finger, to the outer circumstances of your life. You have given your power over to me, or anyone who bumps into you, either accidentally or on purpose.

If you can see this, you have grasped something huge. Your power lies within, power as in ability to take action. Something may happen and trigger a reaction, i.e., the spot, and in that moment, you can CHOOSE to relate to what is going on within yourself rather than to blame whatever triggered the *spot* to appear.

This is true for not only so-called negative reactions, or upsets, it is also true for gifts of joy and love.

For example, if you find that when you are with someone you feel openness, joy and peace, perhaps that person is triggering those qualities in you. Yes, they may be gifting you with those qualities of heart and if openness, joy and peace didn't live inside of you, those qualities couldn't be poked awake.

Imagine owning everything that arises inside of you as yours, the negative and the positive. How might your relationship with yourself and others change?

Hmm, something to ponder, yes?

✍ ✑ ✍ ✑ ✍ ✑ ✍ ✑

Hmm ...

How might your relationship with yourself and others change if you considered something 'out there' a gift as it brought to your awareness something 'in here'?

✍ ✑ ✍ ✑ ✍ ✑ ✍ ✑

7. Responsibility

*Once I took responsibility for my own
unhappiness. I was no longer a victim and I
felt completely in charge.*

Samahria Kaufman

৵৻৵

Responsibility is the ability to respond = response ability. When I am responsible, I am able to respond versus react. When I am reactive, I am in automatic behavior, which negates my ability to make conscious choices in the situation I am facing.

To be able to respond means we are able to make a choice. This is where freedom lies – our freedom to choose. Choosing versus reacting is powerful. This power we have as individuals can make a difference in our own lives.

Often, responsibility is confused with taking the blame. As in, whose fault is this? Once we assign blame, we are no longer in charge of the experience we are having. We have cast ourselves in the role of victim. Once we see ourselves as victims, we lose access to our ability to make a difference in the situation as it is right now.

One day, I was on my way to work, sipping on a cup of coffee. Next thing I know, I have dribbled onto my formerly very clean, white shirt! #@% mumble, grumble.

I noticed the 'upset' and the urge to blame myself for – whatever – and instead, realized blame and upset weren't going to get the stain out.

The question became – NOW WHAT? I have a full day of clients and I'd prefer to be wearing clean clothes.

By the time I arrived at work I had a plan. Next break, I'd go to the cleaners in the building. In the meantime, I'd wear my scarf and I'd be 'covered'. Ahhhh, relief, I had a plan, an action, something to do.

I ended up using the situation as a teaching example in my first session. I revealed my 'error' and turned it into a tool for learning! I took responsibility. I responded to the situation as it was, and creatively used what occurred in service to another.

That was powerful.

Blame extinguishes the opportunity to be creative in the now. Taking responsibility ignites creativity. When faced with 'now what', the imagination is invited to play with possibilities.

We can choose and choose again. Too many of us grew up with the saying, *"well you made your bed, now sleep in it."* Well, you can sleep in it, you can get up, you can make your bed, you can sleep in it again, you can buy a new bed, you can move to a new house, you can sleep on the floor, you can sleep in a hammock. Every night is a new night, so you can choose and choose again.

Our actions produce a result and we can choose again.

This is ease. This is flow. This is power.

Even when we have no influence over outer circumstances, we do have authority over our inner response to the situation. For example, back to my climb up the tree in Chapter One. It was easy for me to blame George (my rope ladder guy), initially, for upsetting my ascent by letting go of the ladder. Blame leads to resentment and resentment is a poison you drink, hoping the other person will die. (Not tasty or fun).

Upset really is an automatic response of the nervous system to something happening other than what was expected. We now have a choice. What do we do now? I moved from upset to curiosity. Do I still want to keep moving up this tree and if so, what is possible now? How do I make that happen? How can I respond to these circumstances as they are in THIS moment? The past is irrelevant.

George's letting go of the ladder was a gift. It showed me I was more than I thought, by pushing me to expand and discover what I was capable of, contributing not only to my life of wonder about personal power, but if he hadn't let go of that ladder, I may never have written this book! That is a lot of riches harvested from a moment in time. All because I chose to see myself not as a victim to mean villain George, but as a person able to respond to the challenges I was facing.

(Just checking ... you did read Chapter One and you know who George is, yes?)

ళ్ళ ళ్ళ ళ్ళ

Do This ... The Ability to Respond

- Remember, responsibility occurs right now. In THIS moment, you get to choose. Your choices and your actions are where you have power.
- When something happens, ask yourself, *"Now what?"*
- This power question stimulates the imagination to offer choices, possibilities, and actions.

What will you choose?

8. Grapefruit Brain

It is not our ability that shows who we truly are

– it is our choices.

Professor Dumbledore

༄

In my work with people, I often hear the cry, *"Oh, it is so much work to be conscious!"* and this is true. The process of awakening into expanded awareness is an ongoing practice.

Imagine the brain as a grapefruit. The juicy insides are akin to the most ancient part of the brain, the reptilian brain. This is where our survival instincts lie.

The spongy white part surrounding the juicy insides can be seen as the mammalian or limbic brain, the emotional center lives here.

The thin rind that surrounds the fruit corresponds to our neocortex, the seat of consciousness for a human being, the part of our brain that is the most recent to evolve, that piece that makes us human.

Because there is a great force of habit of millions of years, and because the juicy part of the grapefruit is enormous compared to the rest, it is easy to see why we so quickly act from the survival part of our brain.

Responding from awareness takes PRACTICE. We need to

practice continuously accessing the rind, the neocortex, so that we can respond, not react to the circumstances we find ourselves in.

It takes choosing, and choosing, and choosing, and choosing, until we create brain pathways that will go to the neocortex for information and direction, rather than the more archaic aspects of the brain.

Yes, this is work. This is a planet of work. No matter what we do, we are exerting effort and energy. The question isn't the victim plea, *"Why do I have to work at this?"* The empowering question is, *"Where do I want to be investing my time and energy?"*

When we don't choose to cultivate conscious awareness through repetition, our energy and effort are directed by unconscious, archaic programming and we get to live with the result of our unconsciousness. We always get to live in the consequences of our choices.

Instead of complaining about the same ol' same ol', we can put our effort and intention into more conscious choices, thus creating more of what our human heart desires. If we don't maintain awareness of what we want, it is easy for that juicy reptile to take over.

Slurp.

Gulp.

Time for a nap in the sun on a rock.

9. Meeting What IS

What we see depends mainly on what we look
for.

John Lubbock

ৡৰ

Sometimes I am triggered. What I mean by triggered is 'something happened' and now I'm upset. Most folks assume, *"I'm upset because something happened."*

What if this is a lie? An understandable conclusion, yet not true? What if whatever happened just happened? What if you are upset, because you are upset? What if the former didn't create the latter?

Have you ever noticed that one day you could go to the sink and find dirty dishes left there by someone else, clean them and put them away without a thought, yet the next day, you go to the same sink and there are dirty dishes left by that same someone, but this time you find yourself upset? How is it the 'something' was nothing the first time, but upsetting the second?

Perhaps it is not the dishes, or the person who left them. Perhaps something in you is upset and has now found a 'something' to attach to. Now your 'upset' is upset by the dishes left by that someone because the mind needs a reason to be upset. Funny thing, the mind.

What if you are just upset? Something is out of order *inside* of you and it is appearing as disturbance. What if you turned to meet that place of disquiet within you and placed your attention inside, instead of on the dishes, the person who left them, and what that must mean about what they think of you, how you are being treated, how dare they disrespect you, who do they think they are and so on?

By the time you get to the end of the 'and so on,' you are REALLY upset and that dirty-dish-leaving person would be wise not to come home any time soon, if ever.

Instead, I suggest you recognize that you are upset and accept that this is so. It's not good or bad, nor right or wrong. It just is what is right now. You're upset.

Notice your upset. If you are like most people, you might feel a tightening in the muscles, especially in the shoulders. You might find your heart beating faster, your breathing shallow in the upper part of your chest and your mind racing with reactive thoughts. If you take time to observe your thoughts, you might notice they are not very pretty. They may look like #!@% and worse. I bet they don't sound like melodious music either.

I'm going to ask you to embrace the enemy within. The way you do that is to allow yourself to feel the disturbance in you. Feel it fully. Welcome whatever is there.

Notice the physical sensations in your body. Where are they located?

Pay attention to your breath. Allow your breath to relax and open.

Observe the thoughts. Notice how they come and go.

Just observe with acceptance. Watch the show. Be present with what is. You don't have to do or change anything. Just accept what is. Get familiar with what goes on in there when you are upset. This is how YOU do upset. It's good to know.

Now ask yourself, *"What is deeper than all of this?"* Allow yourself to find the quiet, the stillness that is present? Breathe into the quiet stillness. Trust me it's there. Stay with this. Be willing to discover what is deeper than the disturbance and notice what happens.

If you are like most people, you will find that the upset disappears. It goes back into the nothingness from which it came. For in reality nothing happened at all. There were dishes in the sink. So what? What your mind created from that fact was what was upsetting, not the dishes.

From this quieter place, you can see if there is an action you want to take. Do you want to make a request of that somebody who left the dishes? If so, imagine asking from this peaceful place. Might asking from peace produce a more positive result than when you were upset? One invites cooperation, the other invites war. Which would you prefer?

NOW A STORY

On a cold, snowy, gray January day in Chicago, I was backing out of a parking space when I suddenly heard that dreaded crunch and immediately stopped my car. Jumping out, I discovered I had backed out of my space as a man was backing out of his, each in the other's blind spot.

I looked at his bumper in dismay. It was smashed, as was his left rear taillight. I heard someone asking me if I was all right. Looking up, I met the eyes of a kind man. I said, *"I'm fine, but your car is a mess, please forgive me."*

His response, *"Don't worry, it was like that already,"* and then moved to checking out my car to see if it was okay.

I thought, *"I just hit your car and you're not going to take advantage of the moment to place blame on me for what occurred? Really?? Instead you are kindly making sure my car and I are okay."* I was touched by this man's kindness and the graciousness of the situation.

How often does someone bang into us in a place that already hurts, and we blame them for hurting us? When was the last time someone said to you, *"Don't worry, I was already dented right there and you just happened to hit it again."*?

Not often. More likely we blame the current

circumstances for why we are hurting, even though we were 'dented already'. It's another example of, *"I'm upset because..."* As humans we tend to throw the cause on whoever or whatever is standing in front of us.

Even if I was the one to damage his car, how would blaming me, yelling at me, falling on the ground in self-pity, rectify the situation? What happened, happened. How we relate to what happened is what matters. Instead of looking to find fault for the situation, we can instead find a way to relate to whatever is occurring with gracious kindness for self and all involved.

Kindness is a power tool. Kindness heals.

Life happens. Change, surprise, unexpected moments occur throughout each day. We get perturbed. So what. Now what?

ꙮ ꙮ ꙮ

Do This ... B r e a t h e

Adding ease to life through breath can be done anytime you want to take a moment to quiet and center in your heart. The technique is powerful and simple and can be used whenever you want to create greater relaxation or more energy.

- Focus your attention on your heart area.
- You may enjoy placing your hands on your heart, or just imagine yourself doing so.

- Breathe in for about 5 or 6 seconds and out 5 or 6 seconds.
- Picture yourself breathing in and breathing out through your heart area.
- Do this for about a minute or two, or even more.

You may discover this type of focused breathing leads you naturally into a state of ease with more energy and resilience. This kind of breathing is a great way to start your day and also a way to lovingly tuck yourself into bed at night. Just a few minutes of breathing this way, will calm and restore.

10. Whose Business is it Anyway?

"If everybody minded their own business," the Duchess said, in a hoarse growl, "the world would go around a great deal faster than it does."

Lewis Carroll

৵ৱ

Many of us struggle with where our business ends and another's business begins. We drift into other people's business and invite other people into ours, all the while making a mess of our relationships because no one is taking 100% responsibility for their own business.

What does that mean? One hundred percent responsibility? When I am 100% responsible for my life, I am responsible for the areas that are my concern: my health, my finances, my emotional well-being, my creativity, my happiness, my fulfillment. I am choosing how to respond, what actions to take to thrive in those areas (as I'm a person who chooses to thrive in my life). No one else is responsible. My life is MY responsibility.

When I make it about anyone else, when I am waiting for someone out there to give it to me, rescue me, do it for me, fix it or carry me, I am at less than 100%.

What does *more* than 100% look like? It looks like me getting into your business and attempting to manipulate, control, direct your choices, and your actions sourced from a fear of being out of control. A different approach sourced from the same sense of disempowerment. Still looking to something out there versus accessing our personal power, our ability to choose and take action.

Imagine being a storeowner. One night after store hours, your store gets broken into. The next day, you complain to the cops that they weren't doing their job and that it was their fault (or society's, or the economy's, or whatever) that you were subjected to this experience.

There is another approach. *Something happened.* The store was broken into. You could use this as an opportunity to CHOOSE to DO something different. Perhaps you might realize you weren't prepared for this possibility and learn from what occurred. Perhaps you would take corrective action by getting an alarm system = responsible = the ability to respond = taking charge of your choices and your actions = responding to circumstances.

Imagine living in each approach, the one where something out there is to blame for the fix you are in, versus the one where you use what happened to learn from and to then choose to do something different. Which one might foster a victim stance? Which one might nurture a sense of empowerment?

Now imagine you are a store owner again and this time, instead of tending to your own business, making sure your store was in order, your inventory stocked, your employees delivering impeccable service to your customers, you were wandering around the streets, going in and out of other shops, offering unasked advice, tips, suggestions about how they could improve their bottom line, criticizing how they go about things. Meanwhile, who is minding YOUR store? You're out of your business.

How often have you set it up to either attempt to get someone else responsible for what is yours, or involve yourself in something that's 'not your business'? Taking 100% responsibility is involving yourself with what is yours and leaving the rest alone. As the Polish proverb says, *"Not my circus, not my monkeys."*

The result of being fully in your own business, is that you are available to invest your energy in ways that will positively affect your life.

🐾 🐾 🐾

Do This ... Minding the Store

Notice where in your life you feel stuck, frustrated, out of balance, helpless.

- Ask yourself, *"Am I out of my business? Am I attempting to get involved in something that's not mine to do?"*

- If so, back off. Then ask yourself, *"What might I be avoiding in my own life by focusing on what this other person (or situation) is or is not doing?"*

- Take action on whatever you discover.

- If you are not out of your business, but are still feeling stuck, ask yourself if you are attempting to get someone or something to come rescue you, save you, get them in your business and make it better. You are still out of your business, just with a twist.

- If so, ask yourself what you can do to take care of the issue yourself. After all, it is YOUR business.

Practice staying in your business. Notice when you drift and call yourself back. You will discover a level of freedom and happiness that you will come to cherish.

11. Energized or Drained?
You Have the Power

If I really want to improve my situation, I can work on the one thing over which I have control – myself. I can stop trying to shape up my wife and work on my own weaknesses. I can focus on being a great marriage partner, a source of unconditional love and support.

Steve Covey

ঞ৶

There have been times in my life when I have invested an enormous amount of energy intending to make my life better only to discover things were the same, if not worse. Often, this comes from investing in things we cannot change or control. Spending our creative energy on *the 'things we cannot change'*, ends up draining our inner resources, leaving us with less to invest into what we can influence.

Some of the things we canNOT control are:

- The past
- Our feelings
- Random thoughts
- Other people's feelings
- The future
- Other people's choices and actions

You don't have to like it and that's how it is.

Getting involved in these areas can wear us out. They also lead to difficulties in relationships. There have been more times than I can remember, where I invested energy in a relationship thinking there was a door, when I was banging my head against a solid wall. Banging my head harder did not turn a wall into a door. So what's a person to do?

We can choose to be powerful and invest in what IS in our control, only TWO things. That may not seem like much. With these two things, we are VERY POWERFUL!

They are – our Choices and our Actions.

Through your choices and actions, you can change your life.

For example, we can involve ourselves in:

- Doing those things we want to be doing, choosing to be on purpose, while enjoying our lives
- Being real, expressing authentically
- Rather than stuffing or spewing, we can feel our feelings fully and completely
- Taking actions in the present that will lead to a desired outcome in the future
- Making requests allowing for a yes or a no, or an alternative that works for everyone
- Redirecting random thoughts toward a more positive, self-supportive focus
- Forgiving, letting go of the past, harvesting the gift and forgetting the rest

- Choosing gratitude for the goodness that already is present here and now

The list goes on and on.

Next time you are struggling in your life, ask yourself, *"Where is my focus? Am I focusing my energy on the things I can influence?"* If the answer is no, shift your focus. If the answer is yes, way to go!

Your choices and actions are what make you powerful.

By the way, just so you know, with every one choice you are really making two. The first one is the choice as to what will you DO, what action will you take. The second is what ATTITUDE will you choose.

It's not only the choices and actions we take in our life, but how we relate to any experience, relationship or circumstance is the experience we get to live in. That relationship can be seen as our attitude. Will we embrace what has occurred as learning, a blessing, or something we can appreciate, even if we would have preferred something else? Or will we begrudgingly do what it is to be done, holding onto resentment, guilt, upset or disturbance?

I know someone who doesn't like her in-laws. No matter what event she is invited to she rolls her eyes. One day I mentioned to her that some folks don't have anyone inviting them for the holidays and she might consider gratitude as a choice. Her response, *"I go, don't I?"* as if she deserved a reward. If I were the host, I'd prefer her to stay home, which is also a valid choice.

How might her experience and the experience of those around her be changed if she went with the attitude of gratitude? Even in our most challenging situations, there is always something positive to be found if we choose to look for it. For her, perhaps it could be found in great food, a child's laughter, or even sunshine on the drive over. What happens in the overall experience when we choose to let the circumstance energize us?

12. What Are You Making Up?

*Life is quite simple when we stop pretending
we know what is going on.*

Martha Ringer

As humans, we make things up to make sense of our reality. Something happens and the brain does a search, *"What does it mean? What should I do?"* This questioning and 'meaning-making' is part of the human survival drive.

The mind is designed to discover the reason for things, so it can figure out what to do. When you are walking through a dark forest with only a sharp stick for protection, this is important. You hear a sound. The mind quickly searches its database looking to place the sound from the past. *"Is this a sound that can eat me? Perhaps it is a sound of something I can eat?"* Important questions.

Often we make up meaning from our survival brain and believe our own storytelling. Yet, just because the mind says so, doesn't mean it is true.

Note this poem written by Sandra Anice Barnes:

the siren sounded

the dishwasher broke

the siren broke the dishwasher

True?

No.

Just a story correlating two events.

In the absence of information, the mind will make things up.

It doesn't like the unknown.

The mind thinks it should know.

It pretends to know so somehow, there is a sense of security and we can be prepared.

Then the mind forgets it made it up.

Whoops.

Try this. Imagine driving on the highway and suddenly being cut off. Notice you have automatic thoughts when this occurs. The mind thinks it knows that the person did it on purpose, is drunk, is out for a joy ride, texting while driving. It thinks up a story to explain the behavior of the other driver. It's an automatic response.

Notice that the story you tell yourself will produce a feeling. If the mind made up the person was being malicious, you may feel angry.

What if you observed the story and then reminded yourself that you don't really know what's going on for the other person? YOU DON'T KNOW. Challenge yourself to make up a different story. Perhaps the person was avoiding hitting an animal and lost control of the car for a moment. Would you feel anger, compassion or be grateful you weren't sideswiped? Perhaps all at the same time.

No matter, you don't know what is true for the other person. You don't know. You just really don't know. We don't know a lot.

What you do know is you had a near miss and as a result, your instinctual self, that lovely reptilian brain, flooded you with a dose of adrenaline and got you out of the way of the swerving car. Now you feel upset because of the adrenaline bath you just took. Adrenaline residue, heartbeat racing, breathing shallow, muscles tensing. Signs of the 'upset' or 'disturbance'.

You also know you are safe.

Not knowing is an uncomfortable place to be for many of us. We allow the mind to run us by making things up and then we act as if whatever the mind has told us is true.

It's not what happens that matters. What matters is the meaning we put on what happens. Nothing has meaning except the meaning we give to it. Human beings are meaning-making machines. Your personal power and true freedom lie in how you interpret what happens. If you put positive meaning on the situation, you will be more resourceful, motivated and open to possibilities.

Psychological studies have shown people who are resilient in the face of adversity have something in common. They choose to give positive meaning to the experience they are going through.

NOW A STORY

A horse farmer hired two lads to muck out his stalls. He told them what to do and sent them out to the barn to begin the work. After a while, he went to check up on them. He found the first one lazing about, leaning against the wall. The farmer asked him what was going on. The lad replied, *"It stinks in here!"* The farmer replied, *"That is irrelevant. Do your job and get to work!"*

When he came to the other lad, he found him mucking out the stalls with great enthusiasm. Digging, throwing, digging, and hauling. The farmer asked him what was going on and the lad replied, *"With all this crap there must be a pony in here somewhere!"*

Same outer reality for each lad, yet each put a different meaning on it.

• Which lad would you hire?

• Which one would you like to be?

We have an incredible power. We have the power to change the meaning of anything. Change the meaning. Change your life.

Make it up and win.

❦ ❧ ❦ ❧ ❦ ❧ ❦ ❧

Hmm ...

What if there is more than one right answer?
When you feel stuck, ask yourself, what is
another right answer? Challenge yourself to
come up with more than just one.

❦ ❧ ❦ ❧ ❦ ❧ ❦ ❧

13. Don't Believe Everything You Think

*When I say not to think, I mean that if you
have a thought, think nothing of it.*

Attributed to a Chinese Zen Master

ༀ

In the absence of information, we make things up. Have you ever noticed how the mind is ever chattering away commenting on everything that is going on?

Thoughts can be quite annoying. They buzz around your head poking at the inside of your skull demanding your attention. They do their best to disguise themselves as truth. Most of us have become convinced what we think is true.

A while back, after receiving an amazing massage, my eyes fell upon a small sign while I was paying for the service. As I read the words, I broke out laughing. It said:

Don't believe everything you think.

Thoughts are energy pulsations moving through the brain and may or may not have any resemblance to reality. Not that I've always been savvy to that fact. There have been more times than I could possibly remember when I bought into the propaganda my mind was generating. Just the other day, I was convinced I knew the hidden motive of another person.

Good thing I checked it out because I was way off course.

I've come to realize just because I think something, doesn't mean it's true, or even relevant.

It's quite a dance to walk the path of not getting involved in the incessant chatter of the brain. It's similar to having an itch and choosing not to scratch it. Especially when the thoughts are like Sirens attempting to seduce me into getting involved with them.

Yet as I hold steady and don't scratch the itch, the sensation will fade and no longer be calling my attention.

We canNOT control our thoughts. We CAN notice our thoughts and wonder about our thinking.

Hmm, is this true?

How is the opposite true?

What else might be true?

Notice how that question triggers another thought. Do you like that thought better? You don't have to believe the automatic thinking that floats through the mind. You can stimulate encouraging, motivating thinking if you prefer.

For example, something happened that aroused my brain activity and lots of busy inner dialog. I found myself having an opinion about someone's opinion. My opinion was rattling around inside my head wanting me to declare it right. It was trying so hard to get my attention, but I chose to ignore the useless information. For even if my thoughts were 'right', who cares? My opinion makes no difference in the scheme of things one way or another, so why waste my precious life energy investing in useless thoughts? If it doesn't serve me, even what I think is often none of my business. It is just irrelevant activity of the brain.

Imagine going to lunch at a restaurant and someone is at the table behind you talking on their cell phone, loudly chatting away. You don't care what they are saying but it's in your ear and irritating. You shift your focus from the now annoying thoughts about the person's annoying behavior and the sound becomes background noise. You find yourself at peace again.

Isn't that what we want, some peace? Yet we can be in the most serene, tranquil environment and if our thoughts are churning away, we are anything but peaceful. So what to do? Don't scratch the itch. Leave it alone. Don't pay any attention to what you are thinking. That doesn't mean thoughts will stop. Nope. It means you'll stop giving them your attention. In doing so, you make yourself available to hear the space between the thoughts.

Ahhhh, what a relief.

This is true creative power. Pay attention to where you are paying attention. Choose to attend to that which brings you joy, opens your heart, fosters gratitude and nurtures peace. Why would you choose to do anything else?

ॐ ॐ ॐ

Do This ... Thoughts as Clouds

- Picture lying in thick grass in the summer, the ground warm against your body, arms behind your head, you are looking upwards watching the clouds come and go.

- Now imagine sitting upright, cross-legged as the Buddha (in your imagination you can do anything). Your breath is deep and full into your belly and then rolls up into your chest as your rib cage gently expands, diaphragm relaxed. Exhale. As Buddha, you are observing your thoughts just as if they were clouds against a blue sky.

- You do not have to do anything to change your mind. Your mind changes all on its own. Just watch the show. Be the witness. Relax.

14. Asking Better Questions

*Depending upon how you direct your
consciousness, you can use anything that
comes to you as a stumbling block or as a
steppingstone.*

John-Roger

৵৶

Imagine rolling along in life and hitting a bump. Perhaps you were learning a new program on your computer and you deleted an item instead of saving it. It happens.

What are the automatic questions that pop into your mind? Do yours sound like: *"How come I always mess up?"* or *"Why am I such a klutz?"* or perhaps, *"Why do I get all the bad luck?!"*

How many of you are motivated by beating yourself up? Many of us operate under the false notion that if we bully ourselves, somehow we'll do better next time.

Not.

It won't happen. What we end up doing is focusing on what we judge as wrong rather than looking to what the opportunity might be.

Let's now imagine alternatives to the bully method. Consider the following and wonder what difference might occur: *"What can I learn from this?"* or *"How can I do it better next time?"* or perhaps, *"What is the value here for me?"* or *"What can I appreciate in this moment?"*

Notice the difference the second set of questions produces. For me, I experience more ease, greater openness, and acceptance of what has occurred and even curiosity about what's next.

The brain is like a computer. Ask it a question. It will search its data banks for an answer. Ask it, *"What's wrong with me?"* and it will tell you. Ask it, *"What's lovable about me?"* and it will tell you. You're in charge of the asking.

Whatever question you ask, you will get an answer. Take charge by asking empowering questions. Asking better questions is part of mastering the art of living.

NOW A STORY

Sometimes my mind gets on a roll with future possibilities that are less than inspiring. I remember the first time I consciously caught myself in the act. It was decades ago and I was just hired by AT&T to consult. I planned to get up and be at my desk early that day to begin working on the program. I found I could not get out of bed. I was frozen. I couldn't move. I began to observe my thoughts. Oh no, I was scaring myself with my thinking. No wonder I couldn't move.

I listened in and heard, *"What if I'm a flop!? What if I don't deliver enough value?! What if they hate me?!"* And so on. I caught myself in the act of focusing on the negative, what if BAD THINGS HAPPEN? Clearly it was safer to stay in bed under the covers than risk having tomatoes thrown at me.

Noticing is a huge Power Tool. When we notice our thoughts, we are able to witness what is going on. From the witness perspective, we realize we have choices. We can jump on the thought train or take a pass. We can even create a different route to travel. That was what I chose. I chose to wonder about possibility. What if GOOD THINGS HAPPEN?

"What if they like me?! What if they like me so much, they invite me back? What if they receive so much value, they tell other departments about the experience and I'm hired again and again and again?!" I was so involved with designing a new route for my thoughts to travel that I didn't even notice I had gotten out of bed until I was in the bathroom brushing my teeth!

I invite you to examine your what ifs. Are you what IF-ing yourself down or are you what IF-ing yourself up?

We don't know what the future will bring. How we relate to this moment makes a difference in how we experience the next one. Take charge of your focus. Put your eyes on where you want to go. Tell yourself a happy ending. Ask encouraging questions. Win in your fantasies.

(By the way, they loved me and invited me back again and again and again!)

ঞ্চ ঞ্চ ঞ্চ

Do This ... Change your Life with a Question

- Get in the habit of asking better questions. Notice what is different when you shift your focus with an empowered question. Write down your observations.

- Turn *"Why me?"* into *"What's next?"*

- Change *"What's wrong with me?"* to *"What are my gifts I am here to contribute?"*

- Shift *"Why does this always happen to me?"* to *"What can I be grateful for here?"* or *"I wonder what I can learn from this?"* or *"How is this situation serving me?"*

- Alter *"How come I'm so stuck?"* to *"What choices are available to me?"* or *"What actions can I take to get moving?"* or *"What outcome do I want to produce?"*

Remember, powerful people ask empowering questions. The quality of your life is directly related to the quality of the questions you ask.

✄ ↄ ✄ ↄ ✄ ↄ ✄ ↄ

W O W

Living in **W**ide **O**pen **W**onder (W O W) is a Power Tool. Wonder opens us to creativity and allows access to ways of experiencing life in new ways. Wonder questions can be life changing when asked with a sincere willingness to be inspired to a new way of perceiving what is.

Here are some of my very favorite Wonder Questions:

✄ ↄ ✄ ↄ ✄ ↄ ✄ ↄ

Hmm ...

What is GREAT about this?

What CHOICES are available to me?

What is my INTENDED outcome? What do I want?

What is my opportunity for LEARNING here?

What is FUNNY about this?

**Are there other ways of LOOKING at this situation?
(If yes, what could they be?)**

How is this situation SERVING me?

What is the GIFT here for me?

What can I be GRATEFUL for?

What can I do right now to support me in being JOYFUL?

✄ ↄ ✄ ↄ ✄ ↄ ✄ ↄ

15. Focusing on the Positive

Some people are always grumbling because roses have thorns. I am thankful thorns have roses.

Alphonse Karr

❧

If I gave you a rose would you say to me, *"Thank you for this stick with thorns on it?"* Even if you pricked your finger while admiring the beauty of the rose, you probably would still appreciate the gift. Yet most of us tend to focus on the negative.

There is nothing wrong with noticing the negative. Negative has its value, as does positive. A battery, for example, needs both negative and positive to function. It's good to know most roses come with thorns, especially if you want to avoid the pain of being pricked.

Negative feedback is valuable if we want to stay on course. If you are driving down the road, and your low gas warning light comes on, you direct yourself in finding the next gas station. Without the warning light, you may run out of gas. Negative feedback can be supportive when used in service to your well-being and productivity.

Did you know a plane traveling from Chicago to Seattle is off course more than 90% of the time? The navigational equipment on the plane keeps sending off course feedback so that the plane can correct itself and get back on course. Even with traveling off course 90% of the time, the plane makes it to its destination. Negative feedback is essential in navigating our way through life.

Negative feedback is different from a negative focus. Negative feedback is information identifying that you have strayed off course from your goal. Instead of using the information as a tool, a resource, the person with a negative focus gets stuck. Life is a drag, and then you die sorta thing.

Powerful people focus on the positive. They hold an image of successful completion and let their positive vision pull them forward. To them, the low gas warning light is merely information to assist them in getting to their destination. It's part of life, but not all of life.

Maintaining a positive focus has other benefits as well. It is a life enhancer. Observe the difference between two little boys coloring with crayons when a bully comes by and breaks all the crayons in two. One of the little boys begins to cry and the other gets excited because now he has more crayons!

NOW A STORY

One of my clients shared a story about how learning to focus on the positive has deepened his relationship with his daughter. He has been working on being less critical, shifting his negative focus, and seeing his children and his wife with greater appreciation and acceptance.

He reported an incident about his teenage daughter who rides horses. She entered a show. It was a big commitment of time and money for him. They traveled 800 miles hauling her horse in a trailer. While he was driving to the show, he began to fret, *"What will I do if she doesn't do well?"* He decided no matter what the outcome, he would focus on the positive.

Well, her horse went lame and so she did indeed do poorly. He excitedly told me his win. He told me that instead of being upset, he looked for the positive. In doing so, he discovered his daughter is an excellent equestrian. Because her horse went lame, her skill became very evident. Since he was committed to look for the positive, when she left the ring, he was able to praise her and share with her his pride.

A situation that could have been very hurtful and upsetting if he had chosen a critical focus, instead became an experience that fed their relationship. He told me their relationship changed that day. His daughter grew relaxed and more open around him. He noticed her smiling more often. She began coming to him for counsel and support. He was amazed at how this simple shift of focus could so powerfully change their lives.

If you want to deepen your relationships, increase your

productivity, and enhance your well-being, use the Power Tool of focusing on the positive. Life is what you make of it. You are in charge of where you place your focus.

It is up to each of us to choose to focus on the rose or the thorns.

ॐ ॐ ॐ

Do This ... Roses Anyone?

Paying attention to where you pay your attention is an important Power Tool. Some call it mindfulness. Are you a person who enjoys savoring the roses or focuses on the thorns? You can choose.

- Observe your inner conversation and notice what you are noticing.

- If you find yourself focusing on what's wrong, out of place, disturbing, without using the information to move toward what you want, then change your focus.

- Train your mind to notice the positive, what's working, what you enjoy.

- When you notice you're not having any fun, you're stuck in a negative place, discover where your focus is. Then change it.

- Take charge of where you place your attention and discover how powerfully you can change the quality of your life.

16. Pebble in Your Shoe

Nothing can bring you peace but yourself.

Ralph Waldo Emerson

༚༝

John Lennon said, *"Life is what happens to you while you're busy making other plans."* And I say, *"Sometimes we don't like it."* When we don't like something, we often go into complaint. *"Can you believe this weather?!"*

Just curious, how useful have you found your complaining? Does it get you what you want? For me, I have noticed that complaining just makes me grumpy.

Yet, complaining CAN be useful, IF you learn how to use it.

Imagine you are walking down a road, enjoying the scenery, the gentle breeze, the fragrance of rich dirt, feeling happy and grateful. You notice there is a pebble in your shoe. You decide to ignore the pebble because you don't want to stop your walk to untie your shoe, take off your sock, remove the pebble, clean your foot, put your sock back on, then your shoe and tie it up.

Moving on down the road, you again become aware of the pebble in your shoe. This time it is not just uncomfortable.

Your foot has begun to hurt. You decide to ignore the pebble because you don't want to stop your walk to untie your shoe, take off your sock, remove the pebble, clean your foot, put your sock back on, then your shoe and tie it up.

A little later, your attention is pulled to a throbbing in your foot. You realize you now have a blister, and not only that, when you were focused elsewhere, it has now popped and the raw skin is rubbing against your shoe. It hurts. Yet, you decide to ignore the pebble because you don't want to stop your walk to untie your shoe, take off your sock, remove the pebble, clean your foot, put your sock back on, then your shoe and tie it up.

Since you are a master of distraction, you are able to focus your attention elsewhere and ignore your foot. Yet your distraction action is not strong enough to block out the pain that is shooting up your leg. You decide to stop your walk to untie your shoe, take off your sock and look at your foot, only to find it is a mess. It looks like the now huge wound (relative to the size of the initially annoying pebble) is infected. You have nothing on hand to clean and take care of the wound and the pain is becoming severe.

Complaints are like the sensation of the pebble. They arise to tell you something is off course and you need to take a corrective action. In the case of the pebble, your body was making a request: please stop your walk, untie your shoe, take off your sock, remove the pebble, clean your foot, put your sock back on, then your shoe and tie it up. You ignored your body's request so it complained louder, and louder, and louder until you finally stopped and paid attention to what it was asking.

The lesson here is to catch yourself (or another) when complaining and find out what is going on. Ask yourself:

- What is causing the disturbance? (What is the pebble in the shoe?)
- What is the solution to the problem?

Then make a request (or encourage the other to do so) for corrective action.

17. The Missing Thermometer

Whatever question you ask, you will get an answer.

Tony Robbins

ॐ

I was staying downtown to support myself in arriving at a venue in time for an early morning start to a training I was delivering. I booked myself at a so-called B&B in Chicago that doesn't serve breakfast but has a community kitchen where you can make your own food. Very European and quaint. It was clear *before I booked,* that there was no concierge, no one in attendance at all for my late arrival. Not only that, my room was on the fourth floor and the place has no elevator, leaving me to take my bags up three flights of narrow, steep, winding stairs. Also, it was July and the hallways were not air-conditioned.

Even though I had all this information BEFORE I booked, and even though everything looked just like the photos, I was grumpy (and sweaty) by the time I got to my room. From then on, there was something wrong everywhere I looked.

I settled in, showered and was blasted with cold air pouring from the air-conditioning vent, right where I stepped out of the shower. Brrrr, what the hey! I looked for a thermostat but no go. Now, I was even grumpier because it was chilly in the room and there were no extra blankets. Where's a list, so I can document my gripes, and so it went.

The next morning before I showered, I noticed I was beginning to move into full out complaint mode, anticipating a blast of cold air yet again after emerging toasty from the warm water. I stopped to watch the internal show as, here I am, preparing for a day-long training which had a big component of learning to foster solution-focused collaborative relationships.

I had a chuckle about the irony and the self-amusement triggered me into walking my talk. I asked myself if I was willing to find a solution to my problem. Challenging myself to come up with a solution, I wandered around the room. Suddenly – appearing – on – the – wall – out – of – nowhere – was – a – thermostat! In my grumpiness, I hadn't seen it the night before, even though I looked. I must have been so attached to being right about the wrongness of the room that my brain was only recording the data that supported my position, thus no thermostat.

Yet, there it was as useful as can be. I turned it off, took my shower and happily dried off in a toasty bathroom amazed by how powerful shifting from complaints to solutions can be. I had a very different perspective than the night before. I actually liked my room. It was cozy, quiet. The bed was amazingly comfortable. The experience more European than downtown big city. Something different, which to me is quite fun.

More evidence about the power of our focus, negative or positive. It is as if the night before I had entered a question into the search engine of my brain, *"What is WRONG with this place?"* and the search engine brain processed my question and produced a list of results. In the morning, I put in a question. *"How can I enjoy my morning shower and make my stay here more comfortable?"* The search engine spewed out the answer to my question. The thermostat appeared!

I challenge you to play with this Power Tool. What if next time you catch yourself complaining, you challenge yourself to shift your focus from what is wrong to how can I make this better. Complaining about what isn't working only makes the experience worse. Challenging yourself to find solutions, engages creativity and aliveness. No matter what happens, you get to live in the fun of creative thinking instead of the grumpiness of complaints. Which would you prefer?

18. Turning Complaints into Requests

When you come right down to it, all you have
is yourself. Yourself is a sun with a thousand
rays in your belly. The rest is nothing.

Pablo Picasso

৯৫

Let's say I habitually complain about the inability to find important papers in my office. What would you say I'm committed to? Some might say complaining, since my office is still messy. Others might say an unorganized office. Both would be right because that is what is. I have a disorganized office and I am complaining about it. How useful is that?

Very useful, if I learn to listen to my complaints and let them inform my actions.

Keeping with the office example, I could listen to the complaint, messy office, and ask what do I really want? What I really want is to streamline my systems and create an order, so that I can easily find what I am looking for.

Now I can channel the energy I was using to complain into creating what I really want.

First, I evaluate how I have set it up for my office to be messy. What am I doing to promote, allow or create that which I am complaining about? In looking carefully, I will discover ways to take different actions, actions that will support me in having what I really want, an ordered office environment.

This works with relationships as well. A client complains, *"My spouse doesn't listen to me. He really doesn't take the time to understand what I am saying."* We explore her complaint. How is being misunderstood familiar? Might she be committed to not being understood and complaining about it? Based on results, it is useful to explore this.

Then I ask, *"How are you setting it up so that your spouse behaves in ways you don't like?"*

This is a powerful question. When we look at the office example, it's easy to take responsibility for the mess that was created. My office, my mess. When we involve another person, it's a bit more challenging. It's tempting to hold the other person responsible for our complaint. Example: He doesn't listen!

My client is a trooper. She wonders, *"What is my part in the situation I am complaining about?"* She has an ah-ha! Because she is willing to be part of the solution, the search engine of her brain reveals a possibility. She realizes she often doesn't context her conversations so he knows what she wants from him. She also recognizes she doesn't set the mood for her husband to be responsive to her. We explore this further, letting the ways she has been with her husband that haven't worked inform alternative actions.

During our next session, she shares a win. She and her

husband had a great weekend. She slowed herself down, made sure she was in rapport with him and then asked if he was available to hang out and talk. He was. They had the best conversation they have had in a long while. She was glowing.

Nice.

When you find yourself complaining, ask yourself, *"What do I really want?"* Then take some time to look at how you set it up to have what you are complaining about. As you do so, notice where you can put in some corrections that might create the experience you prefer. That is how easy it is to turn complaints, into requests, into results. Way to go!

Power Move

Complaint -> Request -> Action -> Result!
Would you rather live in the complaint or the result?

༄ྀ ཨྃ ༄ྀ

Do This … Creating Something Out of Nothing

Noticing what is missing is a way of backing into discovering what you really want. If you know something isn't there, then you know you are looking for something. What is it you want instead?

- Begin to become sensitively aware of your internal self-talk.

- Notice when you are in 'complaint mode'.

- Ask yourself, *"What's missing? What do I really want?"*

- Challenge yourself to discover ways to create what you want.

- Also, pay attention to the complaints you verbalize.

- Ask yourself, *"How am I setting it up so that I am having an experience I tell myself I don't want?"*

- When you discover your part in it, put in a correction!

19. Acceptance is a Power Tool

The secret of happiness is knowing that there
are some things you can control and some
things you cannot.

Epictetus

༂ఇ

Peace is born from acceptance and acceptance is the process of acknowledging that what is – is.

Imagine accepting your life just the way it is, without argument, opposition, challenge, resistance, blame or judgment. It means accepting your weight is 10 pounds more than you would like. Accepting your spouse forgot your birthday. Accepting that your child received a D in English. Accepting that your world is changing in ways beyond your control.

Most folks confuse acceptance with approval, compliance, resignation or powerlessness. By accepting something (a person, situation or circumstance), we are not saying it is desirable, preferable, the way we want it, or that it fulfills our personal choices in any way. We are not saying we agree with how things are, or condone anything at all. We are just acknowledging that IT IS. It exists.

MOST things are outside our control. This includes other people (whether they like us or not), their feelings and their actions. We can't even control our thoughts and our feelings.

If we cannot control it, then we have two choices:

To accept it the way it is, or

To oppose, to be against what is

How useful is it to tell yourself it is not okay to be angry when you are seething? Or you shouldn't think thoughts that have already moved through you mind? Or opposing the fact that your neighbor stopped talking to you and you have no idea why? Look at how much energy you are spending on arguing with something you cannot change. It's like folks griping about how cold it is outside. In all my years on the planet, I have never witnessed it get warmer with folks griping. Even if they are blowing a lot of hot air.

When we oppose what is, we suffer. We can oppose gravity, yet if we drop an object, it falls to the ground anyway. We can proclaim all we want that gravity shouldn't be, yet it still exists. I can say I want to be taller, yet that isn't likely to occur – shorter maybe, but not taller. (Well, there are those heels in my closet...) Why waste my time in the grumps about my height? Might as well get a step stool and deal with what is.

I had NO control over George (remember George) letting go of the ladder. I did have control over what I did next. Though I didn't go this route, my guess is arguing, resenting, wishing, hoping, throwing a tantrum, yelling, screaming, crying would have been a total waste of energy. George was doing what George was doing. What was I GOING TO DO NOW was the power move.

By accepting that there are some things we cannot change, we can focus our attention, our energy, our creativity on the areas we CAN. We gain a tremendous amount of power when we stop wasting our energy in areas where we have no control.

Acceptance opens the door to possibilities, while creating peace with the situation, with ourselves, and with our choices.

PRACTICE acceptance. A radical move, yes, but ultimately very powerful. Discover for yourself how life-changing acceptance can be.

Acceptance IS the process of peace and the doorway to something better.

ೲ ೲ ೲ

Do This ... Breathing into Acceptance

- Every time you move into resistance, take a conscious breath and wonder where you are not at peace? What are you resisting?
- Say to yourself, silently or aloud, *"I accept I do not like how things are and I want them to be different."* You can say the words even though you are still arguing. (Fake it until you make it means acting as

if you are experiencing what you want as a strategy for shifting your focus).

- Remember, acceptance does NOT mean you like it. You can even accept that you do not like it.

  "I accept that I have gained 10 pounds. I accept that I am angry and sad about that."

  "I accept I have to get to the airport two hours early. I accept that I am annoyed at the inconvenience. I accept this is how it is nowadays. I accept I don't like to travel as much as I used to. I accept the situation is not likely to change any time soon."

- Now ask yourself. *"Can I do anything about this?"* If NO, (as in the case of airport security) then release the struggle. Just let it go and breathe into acceptance. (Notice how cooperation becomes easier when you are in acceptance.)

- If YES, (as in the case of the extra 10 pounds) then the question is, are you willing to do what it takes to have what you want, instead of what you have?

- If NO, guess what? You can accept that too. *"I'd like to be 10 pounds lighter. I accept I am not going to do anything about it right now."*

- If YES, imagine yourself enjoying the successful outcome you desire and go for it!

Acceptance is not resignation.
Acceptance is powerful.
It moves us into peace; from peace, we can
access our creativity. Peace is powerful.
Peace is ease.

20. Declare Yourself a Beginner

Do not be too timid and squeamish . . . All life
is an experiment. The more experiments you
make, the better.

Ralph Waldo Emerson

৵৶

I am amazed at how many of us relate to ourselves as if we were born knowing everything. As a result, if I don't do something well or worse yet, I don't know how to do it at all, there must be something wrong with me. The assumption is that I should know how to do everything.

This is true in all areas of life. We think we should know how to negotiate a business deal fresh out of college. We think we should know how to date, when we've never been on one before. We think we should know how to raise children or nurture intimacy in a marriage, when we've just become a parent or a spouse.

Not knowing is disturbing to many of us. When we are stuck in believing we should know, we set ourselves up for misery. Because we think we should know, asking for help, or opening up to learning is out of the question. Instead, we use our creativity to cover up our ignorance.

That's the issue. We're ignorant. We don't know. Ignorance does not equal stupidity. Ignorant does not mean, *"I'm untrainable."* Ignorant means, *"I don't know right now."*

Getting honest about ignorance is liberating. Saying, *"I don't know how to do that,"* can change the course of your life.

Whew, what a relief. No more pretending.

Now you can decide if you want to learn. Do you want to address your ignorance?

Being ignorant is not a problem if my not knowing how doesn't negatively affect my life. It's okay that I don't know (or care to know) how to change the oil in my car. I can easily hire someone to do that for me.

Not knowing how to drive, could affect my well-being and productivity if I live alone, 15 miles from the nearest grocery store. Not knowing how to resolve issues in relationships will negatively affect my ability to create the intimacy and harmony I desire. I need to look at the consequences of my ignorance to determine if I want to take the action of educating myself.

Nowadays, I have fun saying I'm ignorant when I am. No pressure to come up with an answer.

I equally enjoy saying, *"I'm in the process of learning. I'm a beginner."* As a beginner I have a ton of room for error. Since I don't know and am learning, it's okay to make mistakes. Oops is part of the learning process.

Accepting my 'beginnership' gives me a greater willingness to participate. Knowing mistakes are okay, is a way to encourage me to attempt new things. Taking action and having new experiences are key if I am going to learn anything new.

Declaring yourself a beginner is another one of those Power Tools. It leads you to action and action produces results. Learning from results produces change and that change leads from ignorance to learning.

I encourage you to notice where you might be suffering due to ignorance. Ask yourself if you've been promoting your suffering by arguing with the fact that you don't know by telling yourself you should. Once you confess your ignorance, you may be amazed at how the suffering disappears.

Declare yourself a beginner and
let the learning begin!

21. Commit to Learning

Anyone who has never made a mistake has
never tried anything new.

Albert Einstein

৵৵

In choosing to create something new, we are committing to learning. Learning is a fundamental aspect of the human experience.

Just like almost everything else, including life, learning is a process, not an event. We take action and observe the result we produce. Often the result we produce is not what we intended. That would be called a mistake, or even a misstep. Learning is replete with missteps. Observe a baby learning to walk. Yet when we interpret these missteps as failure, or judge that mistakes are not allowed, bad or wrong, we set up resistance to learning something new.

Being a beginner is fraught with off course action. I remember learning how to type. It was before electric typewriters, which was before personal computers. I made so many mistakes, it was unbelievable to me. My pages were a mess. My fingers kept going to the wrong keys, and the keys made no sense to my mind.

Quite frankly, I didn't do very well in that class. I hadn't developed the finger dexterity to become a successful typist. I was very discouraged by the many, many mistakes I was making. Back then, every corrected mistake could be seen. The only perfect page was a page that was typed perfectly. For me, it was an impossible task! Ugh.

My typing improved when I got my first IBM Selectric. I was willing to type faster and risk mistakes, knowing I could easily correct my errors.

My fingers became blurs when I got my first Apple PC. I could pound away on the keys, though keys didn't pound anymore, and see my document before it went to the printer. There was even spell check! I was in typing heaven.

I would get an A+ in any typing course I took today. Why? Because I was finally willing to make mistakes. I knew I could correct them and therefore, I risked going full out. In doing so, my body was able to develop the coordination, dexterity and speed to become an A+ typist.

22. Learning from Mistakes

The power to observe is the power to learn.

Rachel Simon

ೞಚ

Many of us were raised in an environment that emphasized negative reinforcement as a child rearing method. We heard lots of don't do that, and why didn't you do this, and you should and you should not, and lots and lots of NO!

As adults, we still use this method to motivate. We have come to think that if we withhold praise we will be driven to do more and go further. Perhaps you have noticed this is not the case.

When was the last time you were motivated to improve your performance after you got dressed down by your boss or your spouse?

It doesn't happen. Not when we are being criticized or when we are judging ourselves. Blame shuts down our desire to learn and try new things.

There is a work-environment study showing, when an employee is being critically assessed by the boss (speaking in an angry voice); the employee's IQ goes down on average 7 points. That is A LOT of intelligence. The criticism triggers the reactive brain, the juicy grapefruit brain. Instead of listening to improve, that person is looking for the next possible moment to get far, far away from the noise (as in flight, as fighting with the boss is generally not a good career move).

This also happens when we yell at, criticize, judge, belittle ourselves. IQ goes down and we are not ripe for asking power questions that engage our intelligence, creativity and resourcefulness. Powerful people don't spend their creative energy on judging. Instead, they are kind and encouraging toward themselves while looking for opportunities to improve, to grow and to learn.

We learn from making mistakes. No learning ever occurs without error. How many of you sat down at the computer keyboard for the very first time and were able to type without an error? You already know I didn't do it. I haven't found a person yet who did.

While learning to use a keyboard, I would consistently mess up with the letter X. For my hands, there is something about the placement of the X, which is difficult for them. I had to break the hand motion down to train my hand coordination to hit that key consistently without error AND I made many mistakes in the process.

This was also true when I was learning how to drive a manual transmission. I didn't shift from 1st to 2nd gear with grace and ease from the start. There was more than one jerky, bumpy ride as I recall. Now, after much repetition including many mistakes, I shift like a pro.

Learning includes error. Mistakes are part of the process. When we are growing in competence, we misstep, catch ourselves, and go for it again, until we can do what we are learning well.

We learn from adversity the same way we learn from mistakes. When things don't go as planned, we can open to discovery. *"What happened?" "How could I do better?" "Where could I put in a correction?"* These are questions powerful people invest in.

༺ ༄ ༻

Do This ... Appreciate Learning

- Reframing the bumps along the road of learning, is key to making things easy.

- Train yourself to become aware when you are judging yourself or another.

- Challenge yourself to find something to appreciate instead. For example, I appreciate myself for taking the risk that put me in the situation.

- When something doesn't turn out the way you would intend, see if you can uncover a correction to use for next time, one that would improve the result.

- Learn to celebrate your mistakes as evidence that you are participating in your life.

23. Good Enough is Good Enough

It only takes one person to change your life –
you.

Ruth Casey

৵৵

Wisdom grows from harvesting what has gone before, through reflection and wonder, especially when we ask the questions, *"How has this served me? What can I learn from this? If I want to do better, what can I do?"*

While this process of review is very valuable, it sometimes triggers automatic judgments when we notice what has been left undone. The busier our lives get, it seems it is more challenging to feel satisfied. No matter how efficient our workflow systems are, or how much we've streamlined, or eliminated clutter, our lives continually seem to fill up with more to do.

I have a client who is a steamroller. I am continually amazed at how much she can accomplish. This year she rehabbed her office and her home. During a session, she wanted to work on becoming more efficient so she could get more done, because according to her (mind), she was very ineffective.

This no longer surprises me. We focus on what is left undone rather than what we have accomplished. We compare ourselves to some standard of measurement that often is unattainable rather than accept ourselves the way we are. In doing so, we miss the goodness we do, the goodness we are.

- What if you were to give up making yourself wrong for the way you relate to your life?

- What if you chose to stop auditioning for SuperSpouse, SuperParent, SuperEmployee or Employer and accepted that you are good enough and good enough, is good enough?

- What if you learned to be your own best friend, rather than waiting to love yourself until you find that perfect someone, lose weight, or make more money?

- What if you ceased labeling your high energy as pushy and loud, and accepted your gift of enthusiasm, ambition and drive?

- What if you accepted that you are a person who works best under pressure and is most creative close to a deadline? What if you claimed that as your creative process rather than judging yourself as a procrastinator who is lazy and unmotivated?

What have *you* been judging in your behaviors, in your style of expression, which drains your energy and keeps you from claiming the goodness in your life, the goodness in yourself?

When you get to the end of your life, what will have the greatest meaning: that you accomplished everything you set out to do and that you did it all 'right', or that you enjoyed the journey, shared your loving and were true to yourself?

The day I realized I would die with a to-do list was a wake-up call. I was driven by my accomplishments (trapeze, Chapter One) and neglected the spaces between the doing.

We will never get it all done. Even if you could, is that what you want said in your eulogy?

There is no one right way to live your life. There are joyful ways. Is the way you're measuring yourself producing more joy and fulfillment, or are you operating under standards that are impossible to achieve, ever striving for something more, never satisfied with what you have and who you are?

How we relate to the life we have and what we choose with the life we have been given, is where the power is. Where is the joy, the zest, the laughter?

Perhaps choosing to express loving kindness and acceptance for you and for others, enjoying what you have, while you grow into more, appreciating the gift of you, doing your life your way, taking delight in the journey of life itself, might create a more satisfying, joyful experience for you.

Just maybe.

❧ ☙ ❧

Do This ... You are Good Enough

- When you catch yourself judging yourself, belittling yourself with opinion that you could have, should have, ought to have done differently – STOP – and forgive yourself for judging yourself, or judging anyone else.

- Challenge yourself to see the situation differently. How might the circumstances be serving you as they are? What could you possibly be attempting to teach yourself with the current set up? Don't move on until you have at least two positive, empowering responses.

- Now find the joy. Perhaps it is in this breath. Right now, pause, and allow yourself a full breath. And another. Again. Where is the joy? Seek and ye shall find. Joy is always present. Even when the world is showing up just good enough.

- Notice how you are experiencing yourself. If you are feeling more expanded and empowered, you are on the right track. Keep up the good enough work!

24. When you Forget, Forgive!

Mistakes show us our limitations and guide us
to growth.

Marshall Rosenberg

ॐ

Have you ever done something you wish you hadn't? Have you ever spent moments regretting past actions? Have those moments ever extended into days, weeks or even years?

Would you like to know a secret? There are no mistakes, no errors. Really. The only mistake is thinking you made a mistake.

There are only opportunities for growth and learning. Yet, we have been taught that we're supposed to know how to do everything perfectly without ever having learned how to do it. If we make a mistake, we think there is something wrong with us and we fall into judgment.

Did you know how to walk when you were born, or did you have to learn? Did you learn when you were born or did you need to wait until your body was ready? The first time you attempted walking, were you successful or was the learning process one of trial, error and adjustment?

Trial, improvement, excitement, trial, falling down,

getting up, going at it again, etc., until you were competently walking.

What if, after your first attempt at walking, you fell? What if after pushing yourself up to a seated position you crossed your arms, wailing, refusing to ever make another attempt again? What if you judged yourself incompetent? What if you kept telling yourself how bad, awful, stupid and uncoordinated you were? What if you told yourself you would never, ever do that again because it was too embarrassing, what will people think!? Finally, what if you told yourself that you were not worthy of any compassion or loving because you had fallen down?

Silly, eh?

Well, sometimes we are silly in ways that hurt ourselves because we forget that life is a learning process and that we are continually in the process of discovering new things.

So what can you do when you find yourself stuck in a pattern of self-judgment? Forgive yourself. It really is that simple.

The key is, we forgive the JUDGMENTS not the actions. Life happens the way it does. People do what they do, as do we. I'm sure you can look backwards and discover times you thought were mistakes that turned out to be doorways to opportunities, which turned out great. Remember, the only mistake is thinking something is a mistake. That thinking is based on right/wrong, good/bad, should/shouldn't have thinking. We are judging behavior, circumstances or events.

Now I'm going to give you a magic formula for forgiveness.

Let's take the case of the child in the process of learning how to walk and falling.

The child would say:

I forgive myself for judging myself as clumsy.

I forgive myself for judging myself as stupid.

I forgive myself for judging myself as imperfect.

I forgive myself for judging myself as unlovable.

I forgive myself for judging myself as ___, etc.

The secret is to forgive yourself for the judgments placed against yourself, not the action. The action was one of learning. It is the judgments, which hurt us.

Use the magic formula, I forgive myself for judging myself as ___ and allow whatever words or feelings present to be expressed. You may be surprised at what shows up. Don't think about it. Just let it happen.

Notice the word 'as' in the magic formula. You are not stupid, unworthy, unlovable. Therefore, you forgive yourself for judging yourself <u>as</u> those things. You also aren't <u>being</u> those things. Don't forgive yourself for 'being' stupid. Forgive yourself for judging your behavior as stupid. Got it?

Make sure you say the whole phrase: *"I forgive myself for judging myself as ___."* Or if you were judging someone else, you would say, *"I forgive myself for judging X as ___."* The mind likes to be mischievous by omitting the phrase and you would then end up saying your judgments instead of focusing on the forgiveness.

Now for a shift in focus. The next step is to acknowledge and appreciate yourself. Yummy. This time the child learning to walk would celebrate WINs and say:

I appreciate myself for my willingness to try new things. WIN!

I appreciate myself for the strength of my body. WIN!

I acknowledge the improvement in my coordination. WIN!

I acknowledge myself for figuring out how to shift my weight. WIN!

I appreciate myself for ___, etc.

Keep going until you feel an upward surge of energy, an ease in your breathing, shoulders relaxing, a quiet in the chest. Smiling gets bonus points.

Those of us who expect perfection end up not taking action, because inaction assures us there won't be mistakes. Instead, if your focus is on learning no matter what, especially sourced from a clear desire to enrich life for yourself and others. Mistakes are no longer seen as mistakes but as missteps along the path of learning and growth.

When you forget, which you will as you are human, and you fall back into the habit of self-judging, which you will because you are human, forgive!

Remember, there is no such thing as a wrong turn
for every step gets you to here.

꙰ ꙮ ꙰ ꙮ ꙰ ꙮ ꙰ ꙮ

Hmm ...

Are you willing to be a compassionate
and loving friend to yourself?

꙰ ꙮ ꙰ ꙮ ꙰ ꙮ ꙰ ꙮ

25. Hindsight is 20/20

You can live in a world where there are no mistakes. There is just the next opportunity to learn something.

Katie Hendricks

જીજી

Have you ever considered that hindsight is 20/20? It is easy to see choices that were available when we reflect on the past. When we are in the midst of experience we often can't see the forest for the trees.

We can use hindsight vision in two ways. We can beat ourselves up with I should have, could have, wish I would have. Whoopee, what fun! A great way to make a challenging situation worse. Or, we can use hindsight reflection to learn and grow.

For example, when climbing the rope ladder as described in the first chapter of this book, I used hindsight when George, who was anchoring the ladder, let go. Once I moved past the initial 'upset' of 'something happening' that disturbed my flow, when I looked, I realized that what was working was George was anchoring me into the earth. He was holding the rope ladder steady. Using that information I then asked myself, how could I find a new way to anchor into the earth so I could steady myself as I climbed to the top? Asking that question brought a suggestion from my creative brain, to experiment with using the tree to secure me. I pushed my feet further through the rungs so my toes gripped the tree, using it successfully to push myself onward. Voila! It worked.

Hindsight was useful in it showed me what worked and I could use that information to design new actions to accomplish the same task.

Another example is one of my clients was working to take more leadership at work, especially since his boss was not very clear or articulate in his direction. He found himself confused about what was expected or how his performance was being measured. Though he did his best to guess what his boss wanted, he wouldn't know if he had guessed correctly until after having invested much effort in a project.

As we reflected on his previous ways of dealing with the boss, I suggested he ask for a meeting and take initiative to clarify what the boss's expectations were and what were the criteria that would be used to measure his success. Once that was in place, my client was able to design goals and actions to better do the job his boss wanted him to do. Reflecting on what didn't work in this case supported new action with the intention of a more preferred result.

Hindsight is useful ONLY as a tool to learn and grow, NOT as fuel for self-judgment and regret. Once you have seen the possibilities revealed due to 20/20 hindsight, you have a choice. You can use it to keep yourself stuck by beating yourself up or you can use it as an opportunity to practice new skills.

Which do you imagine will make your day?

Believe me, if you knew better, you would have done better. None of us ever hurts ourselves on purpose. We are doing our best with what we have in the moment. Learning through experience brings us to different choices that produce better outcomes, but now wasn't then, so give yourself a break.

A younger version of me would stay in relationships that had outlived their expiration date. I can look backward (called hindsight) and say I made a mistake. Yet the truth is, I did what I did and thus created an experience I lived in. It is only from here I can say I had other choices. At the time, I was doing the best I could. It is easy to judge our past behavior as right/wrong/good/bad and THIS is what creates our suffering. If I knew better, I would have done better. I know I did the best I could. Time to take out the Power Tool of Forgiveness and let go of the judgments.

I could look at those times with different glasses. I can see the tremendous amount of growth and learning that occurred because I had exactly that experience. Difficult, yes, even grueling. Yet if I hadn't endured, I may not have developed into the person I am today. In truth, I learned how to love myself, truly care for myself because the outer circumstances were so very challenging.

So was staying 'too long' a mistake, or a place of learning and growing? Depends on the meaning I want to put on my circumstances. For me, I chose to harvest the gift of my experiences and throw the box away. The box was just the container the treasure came in. As I am now richer as a result of the experience then how could it have possibly been a mistake?

I live by the tenet, *"Use everything for your learning, growth and upliftment."* And that means EVERYTHING. The so called good, bad and the less than lovely.

⧓ ⧓ ⧓

Do This ... Be Nice to You as You Learn and Grow

Bring to mind a situation that might be troublesome at the moment.

- Ask yourself, *"How is this familiar? Have I been in a similar situation in the past?"*
- If so, review the past, as in hindsight, and be honest about how you may be showing up to perpetuate the problem. Remember my client's choice to guess at his boss's intent, instead of taking the time to have a clarifying conversation? Not what I would call efficient or effective.
- Now challenge yourself to come up with something different. (Reminder: The key to success is to do more of what works, less of what doesn't and experiment with new things. If something's not working, it is time for an experiment.)

- Go ahead and implement the new actions. Observe the results. Are you closer to your goal? If so, keep doing what works.

Become aware of a situation in which you are doing well.

- Ask yourself, *"How have I used hindsight and reflection to fine-tune the success I am enjoying?"* (Remember Leslie [that would be me] reorienting herself to the tree to move onward and upward.)

- Let yourself take in your creativity, ingenuity and inventiveness. *Recognize your ability to experiment and succeed.* Take this into your bones. This enterprising, innovative part of you is available to you whenever you are faced with a challenge.

26. How to Do Better

*It is common sense to take a method and try
it. If it fails, admit it frankly and try another.
Above all, try something.*

Franklin D. Roosevelt

৯৫

Hindsight is great as it allows us to see where we can do better. Well, how do we do that? We can harness the power of the mind and direct it. You can mentally rehearse the outcome you want to achieve.

I often role-play with clients as a way for them to prepare to do something different. In the example I shared in the previous chapter, my client and I role-played his conversation with his boss. He went home with the assignment to imagine the conversation unfolding exactly as he would like it if it were all his way.

Mental rehearsal will prepare you to do better.

Years ago, there was a study done that looked at the effect of imagining outcomes. A high school basketball team was divided into three groups. After determining a base line, Group A practiced foul shots for one hour each day. Group B mentally rehearsed a perfectly executed foul shot, getting a basket every time, for one hour a day. Group C did whatever they wanted, as long as it had nothing to do with foul shots.

Which group do you think improved the most? Please guess before you continue. It's more fun that way.

Drum Roll Please...

The results indicated that Group B made the most dramatic improvement. Mentally rehearsing the perfectly executed foul shot engages the body, thus Group B's workouts achieved greater positive results.

What am I talking about!?

Right now, imagine biting into a lemon, notice what happens to your mouth, your body, and your thoughts.

My mouth actually puckered.

Now, imagine yourself standing at the very, very edge of the Grand Canyon.

Now look down.

Whoa, scary, eh?

That's the power of the creative imagination. We can mock up something we want to experience and the body will respond as if what the mind is imaging is real. That is why the Group B improved more than the other two groups as it is easier to imagine a perfect foul shot than accomplish one. Thus, their bodies practiced more success than the other two groups.

This is also why, when we indulge in negative thoughts that predict a dreadful future, we trigger fear responses in the body – fight, flight or freeze – less than empowered places to move forward in life. Powerful people use their imagination to image in what they want to create, thus energizing the body to move toward what they are focusing upon.

The process of role-playing is a way to improve performance. For example, one of my clients habitually responded to her boss the same way she responded to her mother. She experienced both women as strong and unrelenting. She found herself hesitant and uncertain around her boss just as she is around her mother. Understandable. She had yet to build neural pathways in her brain to support her in doing something different. In our sessions, we would spend time practicing different ways of relating. She would also mentally rehearse when on her own. Over time, she found that not only was she showing up more as an adult with her boss, her relationship with her mother improved as well. Bonus points.

ॐ ॐ ॐ

Do This ... Mental Rehearsal

- Scan your mental files and pull one out in an area you'd like to improve.
- Select a specific situation and assess the current reality. How are things right now? Take some time to write it out. Include what is working for you and is not.

- Now take some time to reflect, if the situation were all your way, what would it look like? Once you are clear write down what that would look like. Be careful to use positively focused language. That means instead of saying I don't want X, you write out what you DO want.

- Ask yourself – what is something you can DO to move you closer to what you want? I am guessing you haven't done it yet or you would be producing preferred results.

- Imagine doing that something. In your mind's eye, see yourself engaged in new behavior and notice how other people are responding to the newly expressed you. Take it in. Breathe it in. Feel it in your bones, the way you felt that clutching in your belly when you leaned over the edge at the Grand Canyon.

- Visualize the successful outcome as often as you can and then GO DO IT.

- Notice the results you produced.

- Are there any opportunities for improvement? If so, start at the beginning and go at it again.

- Onward and upward. There is always more to grow into.

- On the way up, give yourself a pat on the back. You are doing good enough, which is great!

27. TA DA

The more you praise and celebrate your life,
the more there is in life to celebrate.

Oprah Winfrey

༄༅

It was close to my birthday and I was visiting dear friends who live in beautiful Sonoma country, just about an hour or so north of San Francisco. It was Wednesday morning and I was given my morning instructions, *"Be ready by 3:45 for your birthday surprise."* Oh, fun!

At 3:45 I was ready to get in the car, not knowing where we were going, but guessing into the city for dinner. I was correct, but only partially so. After an amazingly delicious Italian meal, the restaurant selected because of my love of Italy, we walked to the lot containing the yellow and blue tents in time for the Cirque du Soleil's new show!

Once seated in our amazing center stage, up close seats, one of my friends began to ask each passerby if they knew it was my birthday. Of course, each one paused, smiled, and wished me well. By now I was beaming.

Now for the show. We delighted in the amazing acrobats. On more than one occasion, the performer didn't quite make it and we noted they moved right into a TA DA. Throwing their arms out to invite applause. They just made a mistake and they were asking to be celebrated. We thought this was a hoot.

Hilarious and inspirational. How wise to focus the audience on the fact that they attempted to do their best, even though the outcome was a misstep. So what. They were taking risks, big ones, for our entertainment. TA DA! Applause. I'm still here. I didn't fall, didn't break my neck, and I'm choosing to keep going. TA DA!

Yes, applause, applause, applause. What a great takeaway. When I drop the ball, or mess up, TA DA! At least I was in the game and how else am I to learn, unless I show up and participate. TA DA!

The next day, I was making breakfast. I was going for sunny side up eggs, but they turned out less than sunny when put on the plate. I placed the food in front of my friends with a joyous TA DA! Way better to laugh at what didn't go the way I wanted, than to cry about it. There is always next time. The more I show up, the better I get. Even if I don't ever master the sunny side up egg, TA DA, TA DA, TA DA for my willingness to keep going ... and make breakfast!

I encourage you to give yourself a TA DA for showing up for your life! No matter what the outcome, you can applaud yourself for your willingness. Remember, willingness leads to ability ... without your willingness to show up and participate, aware that learning and mistakes go together ... nothing changes.

TA DA ... you are willing!

Take a bow.

❧ ❧ ❧

Do This ... TA DA

- Consciously and theatrically give yourself a TA DA the next time you do something. Imagine taking a bow in front of your computer upon completion of a work project. TA DA!

- What if you gave yourself a big TA DA just for getting out of bed in the morning? If you get out of bed with a smile, then give yourself a standing ovation!

- You could even ask for a standing ovation next time you serve your family dinner, bring the dog back from a walk, or take the trash to the curb. TA DA, TA DA, TA DA!

28. Celebrating WINs

Rather than looking to find what has been left
undone, look to see what has been
accomplished.

Judy Wardell

৵৵

Most of us go through life seeing the glass as half-empty rather than half-full. If I asked you to list your problems, it would probably be easy for you. If I asked you to list all the things that were good, that were working, your list might be much shorter and more difficult to produce. It's not that there are fewer good things in our lives, it's that we tend to focus on the negative.

Right now, pause, look around, and notice. Notice your noticing. Do you tend to look for what is out of place, incomplete, needs attention? Are you aware of what is working, what in your life you are grateful for, what is beautiful? Where is your habitual focus?

I remember sharing this with a coaching group I was working with. The following week, a woman reported she was amazed to notice the tulips in bloom and spring flowers everywhere. Until I suggested that there was more going on in every moment than problems, she hadn't noticed spring had arrived as she had been absorbed in her worries and concerns.

One way to break this habit is to start writing things down that are positive in your life. As you get into the habit of acknowledging yourself for things well done, you'll discover that many things will shift for you. Instead of thinking that your life is full of difficulties, you'll begin to notice your life is also full of WINs.

Yet what is a WIN? A WIN is a success you have achieved. The key here is your definition of success. YOU need to decide what success, a WIN, is to YOU. One day it may be closing a deal. Another it may be managing heavy traffic calmly or it may be saying no when you mean no, or walking an extra lap around the track. A WIN is a success based on YOUR definition of success rather than evaluated by an external standard, somebody else's "should" for you.

Some only consider obvious things such as stopping smoking, releasing weight or getting a promotion to be successes. Any major success is created by small successes achieved over time. For example, releasing weight is made up of many WINs along the way, as is moving to a new home, as is doing a job that is rewarded by a promotion. I encourage you to celebrate all the steps, all those moments of achievement that lead to the 'big' one. It is the little things, which make a difference.

When we cultivate the habit of acknowledging WINs, we begin to notice solutions rather than problems. Long standing problems will tend to clear up as you train yourself in this way over time. We very often are caught in ruts and we don't see alternatives, but as you begin to focus on what is right, what is working, possibilities open up that were unseen to you before.

Action will get easier and easier because you will know that there is something good to be discovered because you are committed to seeing the glass half-full, looking for the good, harvesting the blessings. You generally will accomplish more, because you will find yourself motivated by the discovery of the goodness, what is working, the gift.

As you cultivate the habit of acknowledging WINs, you'll find learning and skill building is greatly enhanced as action is now associated with a WIN, no matter what the result. You'll find yourself feeling more positive, about yourself and about your life. You'll discover joy in living.

Sound good? I encourage you to write down your WINs. Share your WINs with others. Listen for WINs in the people around you. Celebrate WINning! As you do that, you will discover that life is a good place to be.

29. More on BEing a WINner

Optimist: (WINner) – someone who figures that taking a step backwards after taking a step forward is not a disaster, it's a cha-cha.

Robert Brault

༺༻

WINning is not about being happy. Perhaps you've noticed. Happy comes and happy goes. WINning is about enduring and continuing to make choices to get back on course. It's not about *"Rah Rah look at me, aren't I great?"* Being a WINner is much deeper than being happy with a smiley face have a good day. Real life isn't like that.

A WIN is an experience we create by how we choose to relate to circumstances. You will hear me say repeatedly, *"It's not what happens in life, but what we do with what happens, which creates the experience of our life."* A WINner is a person who chooses to engage with his or her circumstances from the vantage point of learning and groWINg and then celebrating themselves for their choice. TA DA!

To be a WINner means no matter what the circumstances, we find our way through and we look for the gifts and open our hearts to gratitude for what is here for us. Even if the situation sucks really badly, we choose to see it as a FOR US experience, even if we are blind to how that might be, and we open to learn how to get up, how to meet the adversity with courage, how to WIN in the face of what is pushing us down.

Trust me. Empowerment isn't for cowards. It takes courage, resilience, tenacity and commitment to WIN.

No one else but you may know how difficult it was for you to get out of bed this morning, get dressed and get to where you were going on time. YET YOU DO! You did it and that is a WIN! Yay YOU! Atta-girl! Atta-boy! Ahhhh, that feels better doesn't it?

We WIN when we celebrate ourselves in life, no matter what is going on. Even when we fall, we go, oops, and pick ourselves up, giving ourselves a round of applause for picking ourselves up. We can even choose to celebrate ourselves for falling, for now we can see what needs to be paid attention to next time. Wow, that's a WIN. Get it?

A key to WINning is to be compassionate as we allow ourselves the dignity of our process. When we fall down it sometimes hurts. Sometimes we don't want to get up, we don't feel like it, we feel like whining a bit at whatever out there seems to have caused us to trip. All that is fine. None of us walks on water.

Even if we fall, and we can't yet get up, a WIN is acknowledging we fell and there is a choice to get up, even if we realize we, at the moment, don't know how to choose or have the willingness or energy to choose, the fact that we are aware there is a choice is a WIN.

THINGS YOU CAN DO FOR YOURSELF RIGHT NOW:

- Love yourself even though you are on the ground. WIN.

- Be kind to yourself because you are hurting. WIN.

- Comfort yourself in your distress. WIN.

- Remind yourself what it is you were on your way to do when you tripped and fell. WIN.

- Do your best to pick yourself up, or ask someone for help. WIN.

- Brush yourself off, reorient to your purpose and be willing to keep on going. WIN-WIN-WIN.

- Keep doing what you can, including having compassion for the times of fear, anger, sadness that occur on the journey. WIN.

Sometimes life feels like a punch in the belly and we gasp and have to recover. Sometimes that shows up like a big boo hoo, or growl, or whine, and that is fine. That is an automatic stress reaction of the human animal. WINning is letting the energy move through and choosing again and again as quickly as is lovingly possible to engage again in living by design with kindness toward self.

WINning is about finding that place of resilience to meet life's challenges.

Another part about being a WINner, is getting out of bed and going someplace. In other words, you have a plan for yourself, something you want to do with your life, to contribute, to become. You may or may not get there, or 'there' may turn out to be somewhere other than where you imagined. Life is like that. The key is showing up and participating in your life. Another WIN!

What matters in the end is that you show up for yourself. Showing up for yourself means you stand by you, support you and love you, no matter what. This is true power.

ख़ळ ळळ ख़ळ

Do This ... WIN
Watch Me Climb the Tree:

- I used the anger that arose when George let go of the ladder and fueled my commitment to figure out a way to the top. WIN!
- I decided to go for the trapeze. WIN!
- I took the challenge to do something different. I surrendered and I fell backwards. WIN! WIN!
- I asked myself a wonder question: *"How is it I am powerful?"* and let it fuel a new direction in my life. WIN WIN WIN!

Your turn, you can start with today, list a minimum of 5 wins since you opened your eyes this morning.

1. WIN:
2. WIN:
3. WIN:
4. WIN:
5. WIN:

Writing down wins is a life changing tuck-yourself-in-at-the-end-of-the-day habit to cultivate. I have clients who can attest that this simple Power Tool has changed their lives.

It has changed mine.

30. Breathe on Purpose

*After all, computers crash, people die,
relationships fall apart. The best we can do is
breathe and reboot.*

Sarah Jessica Parker

৵৶

Sometimes life is very stressful. It's not even the BIG THINGS. It's the little stressors throughout the day, the annoying stress, the computer not booting up as quickly as wanted, the call getting dropped, unforeseen traffic and more, that builds up and goes KABOOM ... and next thing you know you are behaving as the worst of you. Grrrrrr.

So, what's a person to do!

B r e a t h e.

Conscious breathing is one of the most powerful calming influences we can choose.

A full breath, one that includes relaxing and expanding the diaphragm so the belly can be filled (as well as the upper part of the lungs), which calms, soothes and relaxes.

Don't take my word for it. Try it now. Inhale all the way down into your belly, letting the breath expand into your upper chest, enjoy the sensation as you gently allow the breath to release on its own. Notice there is a pause and then consciously allow the lungs to fill from the bottom up and release.

Lovely...Yes?

Calmer...Yes?

We are much more creative when we are calm and able to focus on possibilities. We are always in the middle of life happening. It serves us to calm ourselves down so we can meet what is with creativity and power.

This is good news, for you can practice peace in many different ways, including participating in the Breath-Work I teach (see info at end of this book). The more you consciously breathe, bringing yourself into a peaceful relaxed state, the more you rewire your brain into one that is prone to the experiences of peace, contentment and love.

31. The Power of Asking

Ask not and receive not.

Jesus

෧ඹ

How can you get whatever you want?

Hmm . . .

You ... could ... A S K ... for ... it !

Oh no! Not that!

Why not that? Because many of us believe asking for help is a sign of weakness, that we 'should' be able to do it all ourselves. That if we were whole and complete, we somehow would not ever need anyone or anything.

Sometimes we think that if we ask someone, we will be beholden to them, or perhaps they will judge us less than, or ... all limiting beliefs that keep us stuck in non-action.

Powerful people are those people who readily ask for what they want. Making clear requests and receiving support are part of the flow of their lives. Acting responsibly often looks like asking for assistance. Not doing so often undermines our sense of well-being and our productivity.

It's important to learn the skills of asking.

- Be specific: Ask specifically if you want the person

to respond in a way that will support your request. There is a difference between asking, *"Will you please get me something to drink?"* and *"Will you please bring me a glass of ice tea with lemon?"*

- Ask someone capable of helping you: Ask someone who has the ability and the authority to assist you. Asking a friend for the ice tea will serve me greater, than if I asked my dog to do it for me.

- Ask until: Ask until you get what you need to do what you want.

If you don't succeed, ask another way. Try a different approach. Ask another person. There is more than one way to get what you want. There is more than one person to help you get it.

You could even ask yourself if you can find a creative way to do it yourself!

What do you want or need to support you in your life? Do you ask for it? If you don't ask for what you want, how will you get it?

Making a request is a Power Tool, a demonstration of taking responsibility. When done with respect for yourself and the people you are asking, it's a negotiation. You empower yourself to reach out and ask for what you want from something out there which could provide.

It takes courage to recognize your needs and to ask for help. Asking is not a victim move. Asking comes from power, as in the ability to make things happen.

NOW A STORY

A friend of mine was preparing for a dream vacation, an African safari. Before she left, she was sharing with me her concerns about her trip. The concern was about the food. She is very careful about how she eats as she has learned over the years some foods, and times to eat, etc., work better for her than others. Wanting to feel vibrant, she is careful she eats well. Well, as in what is congruent with her needs.

The concern is, what works for her is different from how the safari guides have planned the meals. The group is scheduled to eat at a much later hour than is good for her body, which will set her up to not sleep well. Therefore, she will not get the rest she needs to adventure out at dawn the next morning.

Most of us have been conditioned to do our best to fit in with the way things are, rather than learning to negotiate on our own behalf in a manner that cooperates with the larger group. My friend was facing this challenge.

In our exploration of possibilities, she decided she would ask to have something set aside from lunch to be served to her when they returned from the dusk safari outing. In this way, her request would be easy for the support staff while she could dine at an hour that worked for her body. They readily agreed.

Simple solution yet without opening to the possibility that

she could make a self-serving request that the staff could say yes to, she may have resigned herself to doing her best to fit in with how things had been written down in the brochure.

Have you ever done that to yourself, not represented your needs, open to being met in a way that could work for everyone?

Some of us imagine there are only two choices. Go along with the program, resigning to what is, or insist we get what we want the way we want it. Neither demand nor denial work to create win/win outcomes.

Instead, there is a third right answer: staying true from a place of openness, acceptance and cooperation as a way to invite a world where everyone wins, where everyone is taken into consideration, including yourself.

✿ ❧ ✿ ❧ ✿ ❧ ✿ ❧

Hmm ...

What do you tell yourself about asking?

✿ ❧ ✿ ❧ ✿ ❧ ✿ ❧

32. Making Your Requests More Powerful

Life is a do it yourself project.

Dennis Waitley

੭୧

Requests are magical. They make something happen that probably wasn't going to occur unless requested. If I ask you for a glass of water and you bring me one, I now have a glass of water that didn't exist a moment before. And I didn't have to leave my chair! Talk about powerful.

Requests are part of the creative process. They are tools we use to manifest what we want. When we don't ask, we don't get, either from others, or from our self.

Requests invent the future. If you ask your friend, *"Let's go to the beach tomorrow,"* and they agree, you are now spending the day at the beach with your friend.

In addition to what I shared in the previous chapter, there are a few other components to effective requests – requests that are powerful, inviting and collaborative.

We make requests when SOMETHING is MISSING. Like a glass of water in the first example, or a day of fun in the second.

Requests are about FUTURE ACTIONS. We are asking for

something that will happen in the future. Bringing a glass of water, going to the beach, are future actions.

Additionally, in order for your request to be powerful, you must include a TIME component. WHEN DO YOU WANT YOUR REQUEST TO HAPPEN? I want my water now, and I want to go to the beach tomorrow.

Have you ever had one of these conversations?

"Joey, will you please clean up your room?"

"Sure."

1 hour later:

"Joey, I thought you were going to clean up your room."

"I am."

2 hours later:

"CLEAN UP YOUR ROOM!"

"What are you getting all huffy about?"

What was missing in the original request was the TIME component. *"Will you please clean up your room, NOW?"* is a request that both parties can clearly understand. We could create world peace if everyone chose to learn just this one thing! So many arguments occur because the time component was not clearly agreed upon.

It is also assumed the speaker is SINCERE about his or her request. Have you ever made plans with a friend, let's go to a movie, and on the day of the movie get a call from them to cancel? Were they sincere about going with you? Or were they just filling their calendar, until something better came along? You might wonder, and be more cautious about making plans with this person in the future.

When I make a request of you, I am assuming you are COMPETENT to do what I ask. There is a PRESUPPOSITION OF COMPETENCE to every request. I would not be making a powerful request by asking my 5-year old neighbor to change the oil in my car.

Also, in my request-making, I would be assuming a COMMON BACKGROUND. In other words, if I asked you to get me water, I would assume you knew I meant the filtered water and not the tap water. It would be something that was in the background of our relating; filtered water available at the sink.

Talking about water, have you heard the one about one fish asking the other fish how is the water to which the second fish replied, *"What water?"* That which we are familiar with fades into the background and we forget not all people share that background. If you find there is a breakdown in communication, look to your assumptions of shared understanding.

Finally, make your CONDITIONS OF SATISFACTION very clear. Be clear what your request looks like and what it will provide.

NOW A STORY

There was a time when my upstairs neighbor was going away and asked me to watch her dogs while she was gone. I agreed, assuming she meant go to her place to feed them, take them out and play with them. But NOOooo. On the day of her departure, she knocked on my door, dogs in tow, beds, bowls, food and more. Uh oh. What had I agreed to? Her conditions of satisfaction were that her dogs stay with me while she was gone. I failed to get clear about this and ended up with two dogs in my house for too long. Missy and Pooch were renamed Pissy and Mooch and, four weeks later, I was elated to see them leave my home.

To further illustrate CONDITIONS OF SATISFACTION: I remember one day asking a friend if she would be willing to support me in an endeavor I was engaged in. She enthusiastically answered, *"Sure."* As I listened to her words I realized I didn't really know what I was wanting from her so I asked, *"Do you know what I mean by the word support?"* She paused to reflect, then responded, *"No."* Of course not. I wasn't clear on my conditions of satisfaction, so how could she be? I was setting us both up to lose. I withdrew my request until I could be specific about what I wanted.

Remember, a request is a request, not a demand. Stay open to hear a yes, no or perhaps the other person will offer something else that may satisfy your need. Be open to negotiate so everyone wins. Pushing people to say yes when they mean no, diminishes the goodness in relationships and sets everyone up to lose. I would much prefer setting folks up to win.

Powerful people make powerful requests. Become familiar with these components of asking and become more effective in inventing YOUR future! Crafting your requests in a way that sends a clear message about what you want can dramatically change the way the world responds to you. I imagine you will begin to receive what you ask for! Won't that be fun?

৵ড় ৵৵ ৵ড়

Do This ... Becoming a Request Master

- Begin to notice if your requests are producing the results you want?

- If so, notice how you are designing your requests to produce the outcome you desire. Give yourself a pat on the back and learn from what is working.

- If not, look over this chapter to discover what is missing in your asking. Put in a correction.

- Become aware of others making requests of you. Are you saying yes to something undefined and agreeing to something that is not clear to you (remember the Pissy and Mooch fiasco).

- Learn to clarify the conditions of satisfaction in all requests – the requests you make and the ones you respond to with a yes.

- Not getting what you ask for is not failure. It is an opportunity to change how you ask, who you ask, when and where you ask.

Practice, practice, practice

33. Requests Lead to Agreements

Making and keeping clear agreements is
essential to the practice of living in integrity.

Russell Bishop

৵৶

Okay – you have made a request. Now what? Well, the person to whom you made your request can agree to participate or decline. If they decline, you get to figure out what you want to do next. You can ask another person or come up with another way to get your request met.

If they accept, they have made a promise, or an agreement.

Powerful people are care-full and discerning about making and keeping their agreements. Agreements create the fabric of human coexistence. I show up for work and put in my 40 hours, because you have agreed to pay me my wages at the end of that time. You have a desk, phone, supplies ready for me because I have agreed to show up and do a job.

When one of us fails to uphold our end of the bargain, there is a breakdown, erosion of trust, loss of confidence, and a deterioration of relationship. Productivity is diminished and our sense of aliveness and well-being is undermined, not a mood that brings out the best in anyone.

Broken agreements carry a big price. Powerful people are unwilling to pay that price. Therefore, they are conscientious about making and keeping agreements.

Practicing excellence in the area of agreements will contribute enormously to the quality of your life, your level of energy and to the health of your relationships.

Remember the respectful renegotiating process that is essential when life does what it does and you, for some reason, are unable to follow through on your word. Keeping to this level of impeccability will fine-tune your awareness of what you are willing to agree to. Discernment before promises are made facilitates ease and flow in life, rather than having to clean things up or change things around later.

≈ ≈ ≈

Do This ... Be True to Your Word

Is it possible to keep all agreements? Perhaps, but most of us live in a world that has its own agenda, and sometimes life, doing what life does, gets in the way. Yet, there are some guidelines to follow for maintaining your integrity and the integrity of your relationships:

- Keep the agreements you have already made or

consciously change them.

- In the future, only make agreements you want to make. Don't say yes when you mean no. Don't make agreements you don't want to make. No is better than a yes that is never delivered.

- It is okay to make a counteroffer to a request being made. Negotiate the terms of your agreement up front. Tell the truth about what you can and cannot do, what you are willing and not willing to do.

- Make sure there is a time component and be clear about the conditions of satisfaction of the agreement, making sure all parties agree.

- Proactively renegotiate agreements you know are changing for you (versus after breaking one).

- Reschedule your agreements respectfully. There are at least two ways to do this: *"Something has come up, so let's reschedule."* Or, *"We have an agreement, and I'm willing to keep it, and I'd appreciate it if we could move it to another time because something important has come up."* Which do you suppose is more accountable, courteous, and therefore recommended?

- Be willing to keep your agreement if the other party responds by asking you to keep your agreement anyway.

- Keep all agreements impeccably. Make your agreements important.
- Write down the agreements you make and keep track of them.
- When you break a promise, acknowledge it, be candid. Accept the consequences. Let go of justifications, apologies and defenses.

Powerful people make and keep clear agreements. If you want to have more energy, clarity and vitality, make only those agreements you are willing to keep and SAY NO to everything else.

Attending to your agreements facilitates ease and flow in your life. Your word is precious and powerful. It serves to be aware when you give it.

34. NO is Powerful

*Saying yes and no clearly builds confidence
and rids us of the misconception that we are
powerless.*

Marsha Sinetar

৵৶

I'm wondering if you realize how powerful it can be to say
NO? Far too often, we say yes because we don't want to face
the imagined or real consequences of saying no. We tell
ourselves we don't want to hurt or upset the one asking. Yet
NO is far nobler when it tells the truth.

Think about what it is like for you when you ask someone
to be there at 8:00 p.m. and they say yes. 8:00 p.m. comes
and goes and at 8:30 p.m., they show. What you discover is
their yes did not mean yes. Their yes meant NO based on
their behavior.

Why did they say yes? They didn't want to hurt your
feelings or disappoint you. How silly is that? Their behavior
hurt your feelings, was disturbing, or was disruptive.

If you mean no, say no, and do no.

Perhaps you don't know how to say no, or you don't think
you have a right to say no. Maybe you have been taught to

think that if someone wants then it's your job to give.

It may be you lack skills to negotiate what you are willing to give, capable to give, and wanting to give, versus what is being asked of you. We each are afforded the dignity of a process that allows us to say yes, or no, or negotiate an alternative for both parties, a.k.a. win/win solution.

It IS possible what is true for you may trigger upset in the other person. Yet you give them a great gift by telling the truth. If they asked you to do something and you are not available or willing, they can now find someone else.

If they ask you to show up at 8:00 p.m. and you don't show until 8:30 p.m. everyone loses. They are not getting what they asked for when if you had been honest they could have asked someone else.

Which is worse:

A) They ask, you say no, they have to deal with finding an alternative?

B) They ask, you say yes, and don't show up?

So next time you mean no, SAY NO.

Telling the truth is a gift of freedom.
It frees you to live authentically,
and it frees the other person to find
another way to get what they want.

35. The Power of Your Words

Happiness is when what you think, what you say, and what you do are in harmony.

Gandhi

❧

Words have power. They shape the experience of our reality. Certain words can diminish our sense of power, our ability to do. Other words can be used as Power Tools.

The word 'can't', for example, is one such word. It means to be unable. Most often, what we are meaning is I CHOOSE not to. I am not willing. I will not. I WON'T.

A client was telling me that she couldn't get out of bed in the morning. *"I can't do it."* As there is nothing wrong with her body, I am almost 100% sure she CAN get out of bed.

I invited her to experiment with me and she agreed. I suggested she replace can't with won't. She tried it on. *"I won't do it."* I saw something shift inside her. She was becoming aware she was choosing, and her CHOICE had been to stay in bed.

She said it again: *"I won't."* A smile crossed her face. It feels good to have choice. It is empowering to see our choices. Choice brings freedom.

The next week she played with the awareness. Some days she stayed in bed, because she was not willing to get up, she wouldn't. Other days she got out of bed, because she chose to, she was willing.

Notice the difference inside of you when you declare, *"I can't"* versus *"I won't."* Which experience do you prefer?

Another word substitution that opens up our ability to take action, thus increasing our personal power, is replacing 'should' with the word 'could'.

The word 'should' affords NO choice. There is only one way to proceed. The word 'could' expands our reality and opens us up to other possibilities. 'I should' carries a very different meaning than 'I could'.

Should is an imposition, a form we place on others or ourselves. Could is a choice giver. Which experience would you like to create for yourself?

Sometimes we make ourselves smaller by depersonalizing what occurred through our description. We diminish our power, our ability to affect our reality, when we use the word 'you', when describing our personal reality.

For example, read the following sentence. Imagine it is your friend telling you about his sleep patterns.

Friend to you: *"When you go to bed late and get only 5 hours of sleep, you are grumpy the next day."*

How was it to listen to that? For me, the communication is cloudy and confused when I, as the listener, hear 'you' when what is meant is 'I'. Especially since I went to bed at a good time and woke up feeling great. In contrast, I find I am more relaxed and open when it is spoken like this:

"When I don't get enough sleep I am grumpy. How is it for you?"

Better, yes?

Another way we reduce our power is by removing ourselves from our reality, therefore, decreasing our ability to make a difference. We do that by using the word *'it'* instead of the word *'I'*.

For example, *"It was sad"* is a very different statement than *"I was sad."* The first doesn't tell you anything about me. It only tells you my opinion of the circumstance, an opinion that you may or may not agree with. Perhaps for you *"IT wasn't sad."* Perhaps you experienced IT as happy, which really means you felt happy during the experience.

When we say IT was something, we use language to set us up as a victim of circumstances. If IT was sad, then I feel sad because of IT. If I was sad, then I felt sad, and that has to do with me.

IT separates us from our power. IT isn't, I AM. IT didn't. I DID!

Finally, how many of you want to fix something, either a person, a situation or yourself? If it is to be fixed, that means it is broken. People aren't broken. Situations aren't broken. You aren't broken. What you really want is a different experience than the one you are having. Why not say that? Instead of *"let's fix this,"* how much more empowering might it be to say what you want?

For example, *"I can't ever find my keys. I am such a mess.*

I better fix it," versus *"Wow, I wonder what creative idea I can come up with so I always know where my keys are?"*

We empower ourselves when we speak in the positive. Stop speaking about what you don't want. *"I don't want this rug on the floor anymore."* Notice what is imagined in your mind. A rug on the floor. You haven't given clear instruction as to what you do want. *"I want this rug discarded and the floors refinished."* Now you know where you are going and you can design the actions to get you there.

Words can diminish or enhance our ability to do, our personal power. They can describe choices or limit options.

Words are powerful. Consciously choose which ones you use.

ॐ ॐ ॐ

Do This ...Watch Your Words

- Observe yourself over the next few days. Notice how you speak to yourself and how you speak aloud to others.
- Challenge yourself to use words that enhance your power.
- As you change your words, pay attention to the change in how you feel about yourself and your life.

36. Powerful People Empower Others

*Keep away from people who try to belittle
your ambitions. Small people always do that,
but the really great make you feel that you
too, can become great.*

Mark Twain

৵৶

Powerful people aren't powerful because they control, manipulate, dominate and take charge of other people. This is false power and has a hidden agenda of keeping small so the person sets up a false sense of being needed and, therefore, powerful – not much fun for either person.

Powerful people are powerful because they inspire other people to be powerful as well. Remember the definition of power? To be able. Powerful people empower others, encouraging others to assume their full power, their ability to do, to be who they want to be and create what they want.

Imagine choosing to support others so they thrive as the best of them. How might it be if others were doing this for you? Consider how your life would change if you invested in bringing the best out in others.

NOW A STORY

I was on a ski holiday in Taos, NM. Taos is known for their ski school and most people take group lessons in the morning regardless of their ability. On this trip, I was in an all-male group.

There was a big snow storm and a lot of fresh powder. The guys wanted to hike out of bounds and ski a cornice. This was way out of my comfort zone. I was feeling more than a little pressured to 'keep up', especially since every time I hesitated, the guys called me 'chicken'. This is how guys encourage each other to stretch past their comfort zone.

Their teasing irritated me enough to get me to say yes. So hike we did, in deep powder, to get to the top of the mountain, more than 14,000 feet above sea level. A cornice is *"an overhanging mass of hardened snow at the edge of a mountain precipice."* From the side, it looks like a frozen, furling ocean wave. There is nothing below the lip of the cornice, as the wind has carved away the snow below it. The drill is to ski off the cornice, airborne for a bit, then landing, hopefully erect and intact.

Well, after watching the instructor fly off, and a few of the guys, it was my turn. I brought myself to the edge and looked down. It seemed the landing place was waaayyy down there. I was terrified.

I took a breath and remembered the happy yelps of

the guys as they landed post flight. I assumed I was capable as the instructor wasn't an idiot and wouldn't have me out of bounds if I wasn't able to do the deed. I was sure in his contract it said something like, *'thou shalt not kill the paying customers'*.

So ... I DID IT! I was in the air. I was flying. It was splendid. I felt huge. I skied off the edge and out into space. Not only did I land in one piece, I was able to ski successfully through the trees to the place where the group was gathering. I was greeted with happy hollers from the guys and lots of high fives.

I no longer was the me I thought I was prior to that leap. It was time to change my opinion of myself thanks to a bunch of rowdy guys who pushed me to the edge of my comfort zone so I could (literally), fly.

The guys were happy for my happy. They were instrumental in calling out the best of me and helping me get even better. I grew and they did too. A win all around.

What might it be like for those you empower to turn to the people in their lives and empower them? How might the world change if we invested in ourselves and each other this way? Imagine a world where we are inviting out the best in each other.

Hmm ... something to ponder.

ℰ ℒ ℰ ℒ ℰ ℒ ℰ ℒ

Hmm ...

What might be different if you focused on bringing out the best in others while they focused on doing the same for you?

ℰ ℒ ℰ ℒ ℰ ℒ ℰ ℒ

37. So What? Now What?

Follow your heart. There is less traffic.

From a birthday card

৯৫

How you relate to your life IS the experience of your life.

There is a woman struggling to open a door in front of you. So what? That just is, what is. Your power lies in the question – *now what?* Do you assist, ignore her, get grumpy or decide to do a different errand because she is in your way? Whichever you choose is the experience you get to live in.

When I am complaining about, arguing with, or angry at what is, I am dissipating my energy, draining it in a worthless endeavor. Like taking money and throwing it in the fire. Using it up needlessly, in ways that serve no one.

I had a client who came to see me, very upset about the outcome of a business deal he had been involved in. The issue was fairness. His values had been violated. What matters to him is a company that is focused on the well-being of all its employees. The outcome of this deal did not support his values.

I asked him to consider on a scale of 0 to 10, 0 being no

energy at all and 10 being 100% of his creative energy, how much was invested in his arguing with what is, the results of the business deal.

Uh – the number was very high.

I then asked him to consider what else he could do with that energy if he were to invest it in his passion, his yearning to be part of making his world better. Many ideas emerged, and as his focus shifted to what HE COULD DO, his body relaxed and his face softened.

The remainder of the session was spent exploring the possibilities. He chose the one that had the most pull for him and agreed to take a next action.

What CAN YOU DO with your creativity, your passion, your caring to make a difference in your life and the lives around you?

I'm sure you've heard the serenity prayer. It is a powerful navigational tool for life. *"God grant me the serenity to accept the things I cannot change; courage to change the things I can; and wisdom to know the difference."* Let's stop banging our head against the wall, find the door and open it.

If each of us commits to being all that we are, to contribute fully from our uniqueness and gifts, love our self and those we care about completely, we might change the world. For sure, we'd change our personal world.

❧ ❧ ❧

Do This ... Now What?

Make a list of what is in your life that draws your attention.

Examples:

- Where to invest my savings
- My daughter who just moved
- Global unrest as reported by the news
- My sheets are scratchy

So what? For each item, ask yourself, *"What do I want?"*

- To be earning a minimum of 10%+/year
- To nurture my connection with my daughter
- Peace and prosperity
- Soft sheets, restful sleep

Ask yourself item by item. Now what?

- Call my advisor to set up a meeting for long term investment planning
- Schedule calls, cards, visits, emails
- When I notice myself arguing with what is I will choose to take a deep breath
- Go shopping tomorrow for wonderful soft, silky sheets

This is a list of actions, which CAN be acted upon. This is where our ability to change our world positively, one action at a time, occurs. Now let's go out and DO IT!

38. The Power of Completion

*Nothing is so fatiguing as the hanging on of
an uncompleted task.*

William James

ༀ

Powerful people bring a consciousness to the process of completing that is useful throughout the year, throughout the month, the week, the day, the hour. It is the conscious use of the Completion Cycle Tool of self-management.

As human beings (or human doings), we are engaged in ongoing activities. We sleep at night and when that process is complete, we wake and get out of bed. We do our morning routine, then continue to the task of dressing for the day. Once dressed, we move onto the morning fueling, as in breakfast, and then out the door for the next set of activities.

Most activities are composed of smaller activities. Picking the kids up at school is a project consisting of many actions that are completed in sequence until the kids are back at home. Putting on your coat, finding the keys to the car, pulling the car out of the garage, closing the garage door, driving to school, waiting in line, welcoming the kids, driving home, opening the garage door, putting the car back into the garage, unloading the kids, hanging coats in the closet.

Once all that is done, we are ready for what is next. Snack time? Returning phone calls? Preparing dinner?

Let's say for the sake of an example, I forgot one of the kids at school. I wouldn't be able to move on with my day. My energy, thoughts, emotions, would be distracted by the fact that I hadn't completed my project. There is something incomplete. Something is missing – a child! Until I finish what I set out to do, my focus will be distracted. If I am going to be at ease, at peace, I must go back out and bring that missing child home. If we leave a situation incomplete, it consumes energy.

Most of the projects we set out to complete aren't as clear-cut as the above example. Many times, we intend to do something, don't quite get it done, move onto something else, and don't notice that there is a part of us distracted by what is incomplete.

Have you ever noticed a surge of energy when you cross something off your list? This energy was looking for *the missing kid'*. TA DA! Complete! Next! Now that you have brought that child home, the energy is available for you to use in other ways.

People who honor their energy, productivity and well-being, pay attention to what it is they have on their plate, making sure they are moving their projects toward completion. When we honor our cycles of completion, we feel in harmony with ourselves.

The act of completing these things opens up a great deal more energy to flow through your life. Often taking care of a few significant incompletions is enough to get a positive flow of energy moving in your life.

NOW A STORY

I have a pair of reading glasses that I love. They are very lightweight, which is a good thing, as I tend to find things sitting on my nose irritating after a while.

One day, I couldn't find them. They disappeared. Shortly before I noticed they were gone, they were woven through the front of the sweater I was wearing and now they're gone.

I retraced my steps and looked everywhere I remembered I had been during the morning. Nothing – zilch – zip – nada.

That day, I was working with a colleague who was supporting me on a project I was doing. I found myself distracted by the missing glasses. I have other glasses, but none as light and as comfortable, or as expensive, as the pair that went missing.

I kept walking into the question, *"Where are my glasses?"* and off my mind went, searching for the glasses rather than fully attending to what I was doing.

I find this is true in many areas of my life. When I leave something undone, incomplete, there is an energy pull wanting to complete the action. In the case of the missing glasses, that drain of energy was apparent.

While I was cleaning up from making tea on a break

154 • Leslie Sann

from the project, still talking about my missing glasses, even challenging myself to look in the refrigerator to see if I had deposited them in there, I opened the dishwasher to find my glasses! There they were where they apparently had landed after falling out of my sweater earlier in the morning.

Boy was I relieved. Finally, my mind was at peace. When I returned to my desk, my total attention was present with what I was doing.

Ahhh - the joy of completion.

What about you? What has your experience been with things left undone, agreements not fulfilled, calls not made, expense reports not turned in, clothes not put away, etc.? Little actions make a big difference. Taking action, following through, completing what we have already set in motion brings a level of energy and focus that fuels us. This is energy we can invest in doing more of what we really want. This energy feels good.

So give yourself a gift. Ask yourself, "*What is incomplete that I can move toward completion?*" Take action and notice how there is more energy to contribute to what is next.

39. Victim or Victorious?

Victory belongs to the most persevering.

Napoleon Bonaparte

৵৶

Most stories end arbitrarily. The prince doesn't just marry the princess and they live happily ever after. We all know they sometimes argue, but then they make up. Someone burns dinner so they go out. They're scheduled to have a vacation in Hawaii, but there is a storm and their flight is canceled, but they are put up in a glorious hotel and so on.

So where do you end your story? It's the good news/bad news syndrome. The bad news is my refrigerator is broken. The good news is I wanted to go on a diet anyway. The bad news is the fire hydrant in front of my house opened up onto the front of the building. The good news is I needed to have my windows washed.

During a visit to an 89-year-old friend living on her own with macular degeneration, it was discovered that someone she hired, in her words, rookie doo'd her out of $20. (Rookie doo, as in schnooked, bamboozled, conned.) In telling us the story, she became uncomfortably aware of how vulnerable she was living alone with her disability. I'm sure I could embellish the story and make sure by the time I was done, you'd feel sorry for the poor dear and angry at the man who took her money.

Instead, what if I told you that this moment of vulnerability was a gift to all of us in that she was finally, after years of being asked, willing to say yes to community support? Her husband was a Mason and the Masons have a commitment to take care of widows and orphans. Her yes had me on the phone calling the head of the local Mason lodge, who came over to meet her while we were there. They now have a connection and she will be calling him for the assistance she needs in hiring trustworthy help. How great is it that someone took her for $20? What a gift. Thank you Mr. Con Man.

Sometimes we don't tell ourselves, or others, the whole story. As a culture, we have been trained to tell victim stories to elicit all sorts of interesting attention from our audience. As I've said before, how you tell your story becomes the experience you get to have of your life.

What if you choose instead, to be the one to tell stories of empowerment? The hero's journey. How you turned lemons to lemonade or manure into fertilizer? We each have the power to choose where to end our story. Which would you prefer? Victim or Victorious?

JUST FOR FUN EXERCISE: Challenge yourself to turn some 'bad' news into good news just by changing where your story ends. Ask yourself, *and then what?*

40. Why Me?!

Smooth roads never make good drivers. A
problem free life never makes a strong
person. Don't ask life WHY ME? Instead, say,
"Try me!"

Unknown

৵৶

I was facilitating a workshop at the local Cancer Resource Center where I volunteer. A woman came up to me and began to tell me about her journey. She said when she first was diagnosed, she automatically fell into the victim cry, *"Why me!?"* Understandable initial response to something happening, especially a cancer something.

She went on to say, the more she sat with her diagnosis, the more her question shifted from *"Why me!"* to *"Why Me?"* She was telling me she was asking the Mysterious Mystery we call Life, *"Why did you choose me, and how can I serve?"*

My mouth almost dropped open. My heart skipped a beat. I was in awe of this woman, standing before me with a headscarf covering her baldness, the residue of the chemo she was undergoing. I was facing a true warrior of the heart. She was asking to be used to serve in her current circumstances, not as a victim but as someone who wants to give and serve from where she is.

It seems that for some people, circumstances are

irrelevant. I have a friend who also has cancer. She shared with me that she asked herself if she was happier before she had cancer? She realized the answer was no. She related to life in a similar way, generating a similar level of happiness.

It is not the circumstances that matter. What makes a difference is how we relate to what is going on. It's the relationship we have with what is that is the experience we generate. In this moment, we are breathing in and breathing out whether there is cancer or not, whether there is a job or not, whether there is joy in a marriage or not, whether there is a marriage or not. Life is here in every moment and in every moment we can experience the loveliness, the joy, the deliciousness of this breath, this graceful moment of living, how fortunate, another inhale, followed by an exhale. Ahhhhhh. How blessed.

🌿 ଢ 🌿 ଢ 🌿 ଢ 🌿 ଢ

Hmm ...

Where can you shift your focus so you transform your circumstances into a blessing for you and for others?

🌿 ଢ 🌿 ଢ 🌿 ଢ 🌿 ଢ

41. The Transformative Power of Gratitude

My gratitude for this moment does not
depend on what is going on in this moment. It
is the moment, regardless of what is going on,
that I am grateful for.

John-Roger

ॐ

Our brain is receiving 4 million bits of data every moment. Yet our consciousness only processes about 2,000 of those bits. What determines which bits of information we process and which bits are left out?

Our conditioning, experiences, socialization, and more, program our filtering. Thus, one experience witnessed by several people will yield the same amount of interpretations. Each person will process their 2,000 bits and reach a particular conclusion. Since there are 4 million bits, it is unlikely any two people will reach the same conclusion.

There is a story told about the Native Indians who were living on the island where Columbus landed. Because they had never seen a ship when they looked toward the horizon, though the armada was in full view, they didn't see it. Their eyes were receiving the visual input, the brain was processing the information, but the consciousness had nothing to relate the information to and thus could not make use of the data.

This is fascinating to me. I am moved to wonder what am I looking at that I am not seeing? It serves us to consider, what conclusions do I habitually reach? What patterns of interpretation do I notice and do these assessments serve me? Am I omitting a host of information that would lead me to different, perhaps more satisfying, empowering conclusions?

Suppose, upon observation, you notice that you have a history of concluding that you are a victim of circumstances, that nothing ever goes your way, that you are helpless to make a positive effect upon your life. What is happening here is that out of 4 million data points, your consciousness has sorted through and picked the points that weave a story of woe. Perhaps in your life, this is the most familiar interpretation of your reality. Perhaps seeing yourself as a creative force is to you what seeing the ships was for the Indians.

Yet the ships were there, just as your power to engage with life as a creative partner is there.

What if you were to shift your consciousness, looking for the points that weave a more empowering story? Out of 4 MILLION to choose from, one can guess that possibility exists. What might you want to experience instead?

A powerful way to support the consciousness in shifting

its focus, is to move from asking, *"Why me?"* to *"How is this FOR me?"* When we look for the gifts in our experience, we start to see bits of data that will tell a different story.

I am sure we can each look at our own personal history and find situations that we experienced as difficult. It is easy to put an interpretation on it and say, *"This shouldn't have happened."* When we do that, we suffer.

Instead, we can look at the very same circumstances and see how the situation served us, how it grew us in some way, how circumstances presented themselves later that could not have come forward otherwise.

As I've said, hindsight is 20/20. It might be, that when we look at our past, we can choose to see more than the 2,000 bits of data that was the original filter for our interpretation. When we use hindsight, we can expand our awareness.

Gratitude expands our awareness in the now. As I choose to see my life through the eyes of gratitude asking, *"What can I be thankful for? Where are my blessings?"* I begin to see them. They were there all along, as were the ships. Not only do I see the gifts, but also because of MY CHOICE of focus, I AM the one who has CREATED them. My choice to ask and shift my focus has transformed my reality.

We are ALL that powerful.

For example, I have had people let go of the rope in my life. One day my then husband, now wusband, said to me, *"I don't want to be married anymore. I don't know why and I just don't want to be married anymore. I think you should imagine a future without me."* A future without him? How does that happen after almost 20 years of being together, after weaving lives together, dreams, families, funds and more? Just like that, I'm supposed to come up with a new plan. Now that scenario wasn't on my list of things to experience that day.

As I am human, it took me a few minutes. Okay maybe it took a little longer, to sort through the bits of data and weave a new story, a story that moves me forward into my life. A story that fosters joy and drips with gratitude. And I have done it. I can honestly say to you, that day was a gift for which I am exceedingly grateful. What has been uncovered and discovered has been more than worth the pain I have experienced.

How did I do that? I made choices, choices to look for the gifts, for how the experience was for me – how it actually was an experience that would grow me into something even better. It took a while. I didn't just make one choice and it all got lovely in a moment. There was no fairy godmother to wave her wand and make everything look pretty. I had to do the work. I had to make the choices. I had to take the actions. Choices like forgiveness, appreciation for the experience, harvesting the learning, reflecting on the lessons, feeling my feelings completely and fully, allowing myself to grieve, to be angry, and sad, taking care of myself physically, mentally and emotionally and more. Over and over and over again until today I can imagine a future without him, and it is glorious.

Gratitude is a way for me to be in a loving relationship with myself and has transformed my life into a life I can look back upon and say, regardless of my circumstances, this has been a good life and I am grateful. It also empowers me to look forward to all that is before me, knowing that my gratitude will support me, shape me and welcome goodness into my life. Gratitude is a nourishing way to harvest the blessings that already are here and now.

Are you willing to take the transformative power of gratitude, and within a breath or two, change your experience of your life? All it takes is asking some wonder questions such as:

- *How has this been a blessing?*
- *How has this served me?*
- *What do I have that I am grateful for that may not have occurred if I hadn't endured this rough spot?*
- *What have I learned from my challenges?*

I trust you can come up with your own wonder questions.

Gratitude is one of the most powerful forces in the Universe. It is within your reach, in your power, to harness this force and transform your life.

Remember the missing thermostat? The ships are there. Others have seen them. You can too.

ख़ॐ ॐ ख़ॐ

Do This ... Saying Yes, Thank You

Choose to be a creative power in your life. Take charge of your focus and discover how it is to live a grateful, joyful life.

- Upon awakening, open your eyes, take a few deep breaths, and declare, *"With a Grateful Heart I Say YES to this Day!"*

- Go about your morning rituals noticing the little things you are thankful for:
  o Indoor plumbing
  o Hot water
  o Freshly brewed coffee
  o Doorknobs
  o Regulated indoor temperature
  o Family, loved ones, friends

- Keep a list going throughout the day. As you notice something, write it down.

- Review your list at the end of the day. Notice how you feel in your body as you focus on your thankfulness.

- Decide if you want to do the same thing tomorrow...and the next day...and the next.

- Is there anyone on the list with whom you'd like to share your gratitude?

- Take that action. Perhaps with a phone call, an e-note, a card, flowers.
- Notice how it feels inside of you to be focusing on and sharing your grateful heart.

42. The Grace Plan

*Gratefulness is the key to a happy life that we hold in
our hands, because if we are not grateful, then no
matter how much we have we will not be happy –
because we will always want to have something else
or something more.*

Brother David Steindl-Rast

৵৶

I was telling a friend about a situation I was facing and
explained that I had two options. I could face what was in
front of me straight on, or I could choose the Grace Plan. She
encouraged me to go with plan Grace.

Let me share with you how to do that. Let's say, just for
saying sake, 75% of our life is preordained, such as genetics,
family influence, social status, that sort of thing, and 25% is
in the area of our influence. It is possible how we respond
from our 25% sphere of influence will have an impact on how
we experience the 75%.

An example: I was traveling to SFO. It was a last minute
booking which had me going from Chicago to Cleveland with
a one-hour layover and then on to San Francisco. On top of
that, I was in the middle seat in the back of the plane near
the lovely loos (as in toilets).

Nice.

Not my favorite way to fly, yet I was grateful I had a seat on the plane at all. Rather than focus on how uncomfortable I might be, or how loooooong the trip to California was going to be, I chose to focus on the blessing of the seat and the gift of my trip. It was just 7½ hours. Less time than a blink of an eye in a lifetime.

Upon arrival in Chicago, I found the flight to Cleveland was delayed – and delayed – and now it was so delayed it was clear that making my connection in Cleveland might not happen. I went to the desk and in less than a nano-second of a blink of an eye in a lifetime, I was on a direct flight to San Fran, in an upgraded seat.

Very nice.

On the way back to Chicago I arrived at the airport early, open to getting on an earlier flight to find that flight overbooked, no room. Oh well. I spent the 3 hours waiting for my flight enjoying good food and the company of an author and an artist I met while charging my phone.

Extremely nice.

The Grace Plan is a choice we can all make. No matter what Life brings, and Life does deliver, we can choose to meet it with equanimity and gratitude. Just assume good things are coming your way and see what shows up. Somehow, and you can find out for yourself by trying it on, life gets easier; same circumstances, different experience.

43. Coming Home to the Loving

*Your vision will become clear only when you
look into your heart.*

Carl Jung

୬୧

I took part in an extended family gathering, something I was hesitant to do in the past, as I seemed to source my actions from obligation and duty rather than choice. In doing so, I set myself up to judge the situation and people involved, myself included. In other words, I went because I should go. Shoulding doesn't work. It takes all the fun out of life.

Before I said yes to going, I looked at the judgments swirling around my head. (Shoulds are a fertile environment for judgment, by the way.) I realized my judgments were telling me that I yearned for a deeper, more genuine connection with these people who have been given to me as my family. I was weary of the superficiality of our conversations and yearned for heart food.

It dawned on me that I was the problem. (Duh!) That my *attitude* was shaping the experience I was having. My judgments were filtering the interactions and I was getting to be right about my pre-formed opinions. Ugh. (I should know better – ha ha – the 'should' word.)

If I wanted a heart connection, what was I going to do to create and invite that experience? I chose to attend with a welcoming heart; open to creating the connections I was wanting.

One of my many cousins was kind enough to pick me up at the airport. In the car were his daughter and her beau who had also just arrived at the airport. The ride was filled with catch up conversation, teasing, laughter and much noise. Instead of withdrawing from the noise to take care of my travel tired self, I enjoyed participating in the sounds of people coming together after a long absence.

On the way to the hotel, we stopped by my cousin's house. Though I was eager to get to the hotel so I could check in and change for the dinner we were now going to be late for, I was pleased to be invited to see the home they love and meet their new dogs. In the past, I might have been irritated by the delay. Instead, I paid attention to the loving kindness and the heart sharing this stop at the house represented and let that feed me.

Upon arrival at the dinner, my mother's youngest sister greeted me warmly, asking how my folks were (they could not attend this event due to my dad recovering from pneumonia). We both instantly began to tear up as we shared our love for my folks and our concern for their well-being.

The evening progressed in much the same way. The host of the event, another cousin, clearly happy for my choice to attend, continued to introduce me as the sister he never had, and shared how glad he was I had made the trip.

Cousin after cousin, aunts and uncles, sister, brother-in-law, nieces, all lit up as we greeted. I was home. Not home as in this is where I live. Home as in THIS IS WHERE I LOVE. I was HOME in my HEART.

When I am standing in my Loving, all I can see is Love.

Looking through the eyes of Love I can see that it is in our perception and in our approach that real power lives. The gifts of love, acceptance and enjoyment are ours if we choose. We each have the power to choose. It is a choice we make again...and again...and again.

⊗ ⊗ ⊗

Do This ... Nothing is More Important than the Loving

- Notice where in your life you feel separate, distant – apart from situations or people.
- Ask yourself if there are any judgments that you are making, thus creating a barrier between you and others.
- Become aware of how you distract yourself with personalities and behaviors and forget to observe the essence of the person.
- Commit to the Loving.
- Begin to see through the eyes of Love.
- Watch your world transform.

✍ ✎ ✍ ✎ ✍ ✎ ✍ ✎

Hmm ...

What are YOU making more important
than the Loving?

*Love is the key – total, unconditional love. Even
when you don't feel like loving, you love the
feeling of not feeling like loving.*

John-Roger

✍ ✎ ✍ ✎ ✍ ✎ ✍ ✎

44. In Conclusion: The Power to Choose

A truly happy person is one who can enjoy
the scenery on a detour.

Unknown

ॐ

We each have one true freedom in life and that is the freedom to choose. No matter what circumstance we find ourselves in, we can make a choice.

A STORY that was told to me to demonstrate this:

A man went to an ice cream parlor and asked for a chocolate cone. The attendant informed him that they were currently out of chocolate. Rather than get annoyed, angry, belligerent, sad, he chose to order strawberry. When he received the cone his response was, *"Thank you, I will enjoy this strawberry cone."*

Even when it seems we cannot have what we want, we can always choose to accept what we have, even to want what is available.

Life has ease to it when we work through the options we have and make choices with affirmation rather than grudging resignation. The man with the ice cream made a conscious choice to enjoy an unexpected alternative. He could also have chosen to pursue his desire for chocolate by visiting another ice cream parlor. The decision is not nearly as important as the attitude with which he approached the result. The power was in making his choice with positive intention.

Powerful people live by design. We shape the experience we have of our life through our choices and our actions. Every choice, every action, has a consequence. This is how we create. We choose, we act, and we observe the results of our actions. We evaluate those results, make new choices and take new action. How we choose to respond, what actions we take, will chart the course of our lives.

Life is a series of choices and actions. I encourage you to challenge yourself to become aware of the choices you make day-to-day, hour-to-hour, moment-to-moment. You could take time at the end of each day to notice how your day was affected by the choices you made. This simple process will bring to your awareness what is working and what is not. You might take stock and realize you have habits that make your choices for you, such as staying up late so you are rushed in the morning and often late to work. Noticing that might inspire you to lay your clothes out the night before so your morning flows more easily.

When you become aware of feeling helpless, stuck or powerless, ask yourself *"What are my choices in this moment, right now?"* Listen to what is revealed, make a choice, take an action and notice if you experience more of your power. The gift of paying attention is that you get to live in the consequences of your choices; not good, bad, right or wrong, just what is. If you like your consequences, enjoy them. If not, appreciate that you get to make new choices and take new action. Learn how to do this well, enjoy the process as it unfolds, and you will be a powerful person who makes things easy.

Remember, practice doesn't make perfect. Practice makes better and better and even better. Choose which tools you want to play with and apply them consistently. In a year from now, you will look back and go *"wow!"* You deserve WOW.

We are mostly traveling from here to there in our lives. Moments of achievement are moments thus fleeting. The bulk of life is made up of the in-between times. Have fun, enjoy, savor, and laugh. There is just this breath, and then this one, and now this one.

Make good use of this manual and use it as a guide to navigate whatever the trees are in your life. May you know that no matter what you do, jump for the bar or fall backwards, you will reach the ground, you will be caught, and you will be held. TA DA! Celebrate yourself for your willingness to show up, participate, take risks and experiment; contributing to you becoming a person living by design, empowered and in action, creating a joyful, happy life.

No one can do it for you. You're it. I applaud you every step of the way.

✄ ✃ ✄ ✃ ✄ ✃ ✄ ✃

Hmm ...

What will you DO (choices and actions)
now that you have completed this book?

✄ ✃ ✄ ✃ ✄ ✃ ✄ ✃

Acknowledgments

Lynda Otte, my treasured assistant, now dear friend, has been by my side, encouraging me onward, there for me, steadfast, reliable, competent and true. Without her support on so many levels this book would not be.

America Martinez, who years ago casually asked me if I was writing, surprising me that anyone thought I had anything to say worth writing about. Quietly and graciously, she has encouraged me these many years.

Ron and Mary Hulnick, founders of the University of Santa Monica, for assigning me a life changing project that I used to awaken the writer in me. Thank you, Mary, for your gentle power; and Ron, for your encouragement to go out and get published.

Gratitude to the readers of my Living by Design Tips eZine, which I have been writing for near 15 years, who have been clamoring for a book such as this.

Rick Kantor, Russ Schoen for their creative contribution. John Hagelberg, Robert McCreight, encouragers extraordinaire. Marla Kraus, Marian Bateman, Susie and Otto Collins, for their patience, friendship and loving, each cheering me on. Ken Benjamin, David Elliott, part of the fabric of support that held me as I moved forward.

Allie Benjamin for making an invaluable contribution to the completion of this project.

Christopher Podhola who did a final polish. I trust you can see yourself in the shine.

Michael Taft who challenged me to commit to completion, therefore pushing me out of the nest. Am I flying?

And finally, gratitude to George, the man who let go of the rope. Thank you for daring me to see myself through new eyes. That moment was a life changer.

Now Do This ... Take a Next Action

LIVING BY DESIGN TIPS

Sign up for my Living by Design Tips, Practical Tools for Everyday Living, an online newsletter delivered to your inbox with your permission. In addition to receiving the Living by Design Tips eZine, which is filled with even more mind-shifting, heart-lifting Power Tools, you will also receive a gift from me, something to support you in living by design rather than by default.

> *"I love how you put the truth of things into ordinary human understanding! You give tips people can relate to in their every day lives – topics to think about – and the humor is fun!"* – Kris

> *"Thank you Leslie! You have once again made me paranoid that you have a microphone hidden nearby when I start complaining about my life!! You somehow ALWAYS seem to say just what I need to hear, just when I need to hear it."* – Bob

LIVE AND ONLINE LEARNING EXPERIENCES

Live and online learning experiences are posted at my website. Tips subscribers will be notified of these events.

www.living-bydesign.com

❧ ❧ ❧

BREATHE INTO PEACE

I trust you noticed that woven throughout this book there has been a focus on conscious breathing. I have found the breath to be one of the Big Power Tools we have in transforming our lives, so much so, that I teach a breathing practice to my clients to support them in resolving issues and accessing their inner resources of strength and courage.

This type of BreathWork is powerful in that it rewires the brain so you have greater access to human creativity and resourcefulness (rind as in grapefruit) with increased ease in bypassing the survival brain (juicy pulp).

Breathe into Peace is an at home BreathWork meditation and includes two meditation tracks.

(Private BreathWork sessions also available and can be facilitated in person, via videoconference or by phone. www.breathworkwithleslie.com)

"You are in my head now! Your voice is like an anti-anxiety calming agent. I have been using your meditation audio every day for two weeks now. I am amazed how easily it is to bring myself to calm with my breath now even when I'm not doing one of the meditation sessions." – Tami

www.breathworkwithleslie.com/audio

๛ ๏ ๛

YOU ARE WELCOME TO WRITE TO ME

I am interested in your successes! Write to me and share WINS you have experienced using any of the tools I have shared. (Ask my clients, I LOVE WINS!) Tell me which strategies have worked and what occurred.

Send your story to me at: leslie@living-bydesign.com

Thank you.

❧   ❧   ❧

About the Author

૭୧

Leslie Sann is an innovative and inspired mentor, teacher and coach. She is the founder of Living by Design, an educational coaching organization. Her focus is the training and development of individuals and groups in the art of successful living.

Throughout the past 25+ years, through her teaching, writing and coaching, Leslie has helped change the way people experience who they are and what they can do. Her clients' lives are transformed as they learn to live by design rather than by default, by choice rather than by chance, while living their heart dreams into their world. She believes living a life we love heals the heart, connects us to our joy and makes the world a better place for all of us.

Leslie also designs and facilitates personal development workshops and business trainings. These trainings foster high performing teams, communication skills and personal effectiveness in relationships. Additionally she speaks on the topics addressed in this book. Please contact her at leslie@living-bydesign.com.

૭୧ ૭୧ ૭୧

www.living-bydesign.com